MATHS MANIA
TIMES TABLES

TIMED TESTS

2, 5 AND 10X TABLE

Multiplication Mania!

Timed Tests for the 2x, 5x, and 10x Tables.

COVER AND ILLUSTRATIONS BY CANVA

ISBN: 9798879528657

LIBRARY OF CONGRESS CATALOGUING-IN-PUBLICATION DATA

REVIEW

Leave Your Mark with Sakura Learning!

Thank you for choosing our Super Times Tables Book! We're excited to be part of your child's journey to mastering times tables from 1-12. Scan the QR code below to leave a review and help other parents choose the best educational resources!

Your review matters! It guides parents, motivates our team, drives continuous improvement, and builds a supportive community. Together, let's empower children to excel in maths and love learning!

Scan the QR code to leave your review now!

TABLE OF CONTENTS

TABLE OF CONTENTS CONTINUED

TABLE OF CONTENTS CONTINUED

Book 3 4, 7 and 8 Times Tables.	
Introduction	97
Times Tables 1-12	98
4x Table	99
7x Table	100
8x Table	101
Instructions for the Grids	103
How to use the Grid	104
Instructions for Self-Assessing	105
How to use Self Assessment	106
Grid 1/Answers/Self Assessment	107-109
Grid 2/Answers/Self Assessment	110-112
Grid 3/Answers/Self Assessment	113-115
Grid 4/Answers/Self Assessment	116-118
Grid 5/Answers/Self Assessment	119-121
Grid 6/Answers/Self Assessment	122-124
Grid 7/Answers/Self Assessment	125-127
Grid 8/Answers/Self Assessment	128-130
Grid 9/Answers/Self Assessment	131-133
Grid 10/Answers/Self Assessment	134-136
Grid 11/Answers/Self Assessment	137-139
Grid 12/Self Assessment	140-143

TABLE OF CONTENTS CONTINUED

TABLE OF CONTENTS CONTINUED

INTRODUCTION

Hey there! 🚀 Are you ready to blast off into the amazing world of multiplication? Think of each multiplication as a key 🔑 unlocking magical secrets in a cosmic treasure hunt!

Times tables make maths a breeze, turning it into a fun adventure! They're like a secret passage to figuring out how many cookies 🍪 you'll devour in a week if you eat 3 a day. It's like adding, but with turbo speed!

The grids in this book 📖 are like a mental gym 🧠! They'll train you to zoom through numbers like a pro. Practicing them is like learning a catchy tune 🎵, and racing against the clock ⏱️ adds a thrilling twist!

These grids hold the key to becoming a maths superhero. And the best part? You're your own guide! With each 'self-assessment', you'll be uncovering clues 🔍 to your maths superpowers. Mistakes aren't defeat; they're just stepping stones to mastering maths.

So buckle up and get ready for an epic journey through the universe of numbers, and awaken the maths wizard within you! ✨

Times Tables 1-12

1

$1 \times 1 = 1$
$1 \times 2 = 2$
$1 \times 3 = 3$
$1 \times 4 = 4$
$1 \times 5 = 5$
$1 \times 6 = 6$
$1 \times 7 = 7$
$1 \times 8 = 8$
$1 \times 9 = 9$
$1 \times 10 = 10$
$1 \times 11 = 11$
$1 \times 12 = 12$

2

$2 \times 1 = 2$
$2 \times 2 = 4$
$2 \times 3 = 6$
$2 \times 4 = 8$
$2 \times 5 = 10$
$2 \times 6 = 12$
$2 \times 7 = 14$
$2 \times 8 = 16$
$2 \times 9 = 18$
$2 \times 10 = 20$
$2 \times 11 = 22$
$2 \times 12 = 24$

3

$3 \times 1 = 3$
$3 \times 2 = 6$
$3 \times 3 = 9$
$3 \times 4 = 12$
$3 \times 5 = 15$
$3 \times 6 = 18$
$3 \times 7 = 21$
$3 \times 8 = 24$
$3 \times 9 = 27$
$3 \times 10 = 30$
$3 \times 11 = 33$
$3 \times 12 = 36$

4

$4 \times 1 = 4$
$4 \times 2 = 8$
$4 \times 3 = 12$
$4 \times 4 = 16$
$4 \times 5 = 20$
$4 \times 6 = 24$
$4 \times 7 = 28$
$4 \times 8 = 32$
$4 \times 9 = 36$
$4 \times 10 = 40$
$4 \times 11 = 44$
$4 \times 12 = 48$

5

$5 \times 1 = 5$
$5 \times 2 = 10$
$5 \times 3 = 15$
$5 \times 4 = 20$
$5 \times 5 = 25$
$5 \times 6 = 30$
$5 \times 7 = 35$
$5 \times 8 = 40$
$5 \times 9 = 45$
$5 \times 10 = 50$
$5 \times 11 = 55$
$5 \times 12 = 60$

6

$6 \times 1 = 6$
$6 \times 2 = 12$
$6 \times 3 = 18$
$6 \times 4 = 24$
$6 \times 5 = 30$
$6 \times 6 = 36$
$6 \times 7 = 42$
$6 \times 8 = 48$
$6 \times 9 = 54$
$6 \times 10 = 60$
$6 \times 11 = 66$
$6 \times 12 = 72$

7

$7 \times 1 = 7$
$7 \times 2 = 14$
$7 \times 3 = 21$
$7 \times 4 = 28$
$7 \times 5 = 35$
$7 \times 6 = 42$
$7 \times 7 = 49$
$7 \times 8 = 56$
$7 \times 9 = 63$
$7 \times 10 = 70$
$7 \times 11 = 77$
$7 \times 12 = 84$

8

$8 \times 1 = 8$
$8 \times 2 = 16$
$8 \times 3 = 24$
$8 \times 4 = 32$
$8 \times 5 = 40$
$8 \times 6 = 48$
$8 \times 7 = 56$
$8 \times 8 = 64$
$8 \times 9 = 72$
$8 \times 10 = 80$
$8 \times 11 = 88$
$8 \times 12 = 96$

9

$9 \times 1 = 9$
$9 \times 2 = 18$
$9 \times 3 = 27$
$9 \times 4 = 36$
$9 \times 5 = 45$
$9 \times 6 = 54$
$9 \times 7 = 63$
$9 \times 8 = 72$
$9 \times 9 = 81$
$9 \times 10 = 90$
$9 \times 11 = 99$
$9 \times 12 = 108$

10

$10 \times 1 = 10$
$10 \times 2 = 20$
$10 \times 3 = 30$
$10 \times 4 = 40$
$10 \times 5 = 50$
$10 \times 6 = 60$
$10 \times 7 = 70$
$10 \times 8 = 80$
$10 \times 9 = 90$
$10 \times 10 = 100$
$10 \times 11 = 110$
$10 \times 12 = 120$

11

$11 \times 1 = 11$
$11 \times 2 = 22$
$11 \times 3 = 33$
$11 \times 4 = 44$
$11 \times 5 = 55$
$11 \times 6 = 66$
$11 \times 7 = 77$
$11 \times 8 = 88$
$11 \times 9 = 99$
$11 \times 10 = 110$
$11 \times 11 = 121$
$11 \times 12 = 132$

12

$12 \times 1 = 12$
$12 \times 2 = 24$
$12 \times 3 = 36$
$12 \times 4 = 48$
$12 \times 5 = 60$
$12 \times 6 = 72$
$12 \times 7 = 84$
$12 \times 8 = 96$
$12 \times 9 = 108$
$12 \times 10 = 120$
$12 \times 11 = 132$
$12 \times 12 = 144$

2 x Table

1 X 2 = 2

2 X 2 = 4

3 X 2 = 6

4 X 2 = 8

5 X 2 = 10

6 X 2 = 12

7 X 2 = 14

8 X 2 = 16

9 X 2 = 18

10 X 2 = 20

11 x 2 = 22

12 x 2 = 24

5 x Table

1 X 5 = 5
2 X 5 = 10
3 X 5 = 15
4 X 5 = 20
5 X 5 = 25
6 X 5 = 30
7 X 5 = 35
8 X 5 = 40
9 X 5 = 45
10 X 5 = 50
11 x 5 = 55
12 x 5 = 60

10 x Table

1 X 10 = 10

2 X 10 = 20

3 X 10 = 30

4 X 10 = 40

5 X 10 = 50

6 X 10 = 60

7 X 10 = 70

8 X 10 = 80

9 X 10 = 90

10 X 10 = 100

11 x 10 = 110

12 x 10 = 120

TIMES TABLES GRIDS

INSTRUCTIONS FOR THE GRIDS

Get ready for a thrilling math ride! We're mastering times tables for the 2, 5 and 10 times tables with a magic grid, uncovering hidden treasures of knowledge! ✦

1️⃣ Prep your grid! Imagine each row and column as pathways to secret answers.

2️⃣ Pick a number, find its row, then glide down to meet another number's column. Multiply! You're a number explorer now! 🔍

3️⃣ Found the spot where row and column intersect? There's your treasure! Jot down that precious number.

4️⃣ Time for detective work! 🕵️ Scrutinize your grid, celebrate correct answers with ticks (✔), and mark areas for improvement with a splash of colour.

Ready to conquer those tables? Dive in! Need help? Answers are hidden at the back of this first book—no peeking at other grids! 🙈 Let the maths adventure begin! 🚀

For a clear guide, flip to the next page to see a diagram with step-by-step instructions! Happy exploring!

HOW TO USE THE GRID

Example			
x	2	5	10
1	2	5	10
2	4	10	20
3	6	15	30
4	8	20	40
5	10	24	50
6	12	30	60
7	14	35	70
8	16	40	80
9	17	45	90
10	20	50	100
11	22	55	110
12	24	50	120
Total	12	12	12
Time = 10mins 20secs		Total = 36	

SPOT THE SLIP-UP, SO YOU CAN PERFECT IT NEXT TIME.

TALLY UP YOUR SCORE AND JOT IT DOWN!

CLOCK IN YOUR GRID COMPLETION TIME.

8

INSTRUCTIONS FOR SELF-ASSESSING

Let's dive into the exciting part - Self-Assessment, Reflection, and Goal-Setting! 🚀 Use your colouring pens 🖍 to fill in stars and faces, showing your mastery over each question. More happy faces, more power to you! ☺

Check off ☑ you understood times tables, and note the tricky ones 🔧. With a bit of help, set your improvement goals in the final box. Remember, setting goals is your roadmap to success!

Embrace the Marvellous Mistake Mission! Choose three notable errors and rewrite each five times. Focus prevents confusion and turns blunders into wisdom! Stuck? Set a new mini-goal! It's self-coaching towards mastering, say, the 5 times table. 🏃

By acknowledging mistakes, practicing, and goal-setting, you're stepping into your maths magician shoes! 🎩✨ Your colourful corrections and highlights will make your learning journey shine! ⭐ Ready to be a multiplication master? The adventure awaits! 🌈

HOW TO USE SELF-ASSESSMENT

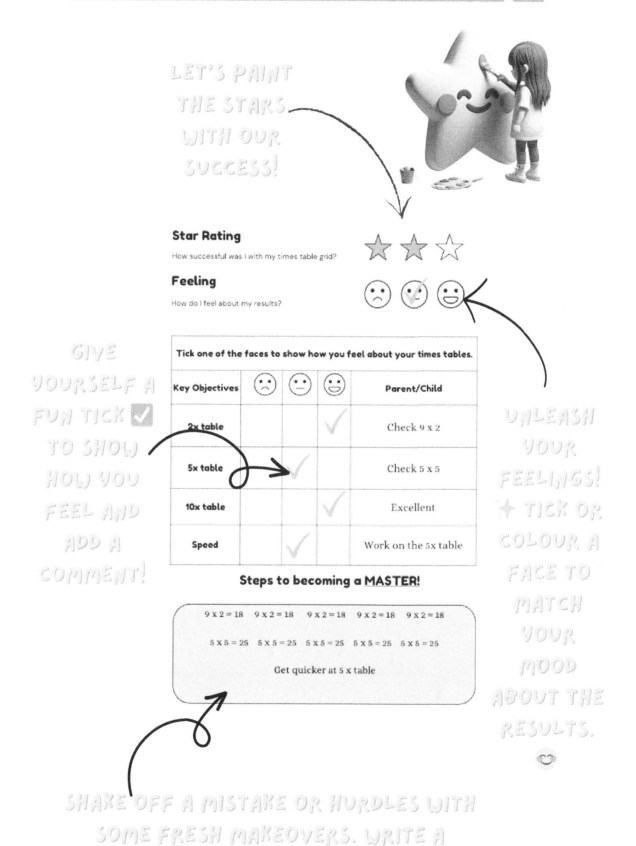

LET'S PAINT
THE STARS
WITH OUR
SUCCESS!

Star Rating

How successful was I with my times table grid?

Feeling

How do I feel about my results?

GIVE
YOURSELF A
FUN TICK ✅
TO SHOW
HOW YOU
FEEL AND
ADD A
COMMENT!

Tick one of the faces to show how you feel about your times tables.

Key Objectives	☹	😐	😊	Parent/Child
2x table			✓	Check 9 x 2
5x table		✓		Check 5 x 5
10x table			✓	Excellent
Speed		✓		Work on the 5x table

Steps to becoming a MASTER!

9 x 2 = 18   9 x 2 = 18   9 x 2 = 18   9 x 2 = 18   9 x 2 = 18

5 X 5 = 25   5 X 5 = 25   5 X 5 = 25   5 X 5 = 25   5 X 5 = 25

Get quicker at 5 x table

UNLEASH
YOUR
FEELINGS!
✦ TICK OR
COLOUR A
FACE TO
MATCH
YOUR
MOOD
ABOUT THE
RESULTS.
😊

SHAKE OFF A MISTAKE OR HURDLES WITH
SOME FRESH MAKEOVERS. WRITE A
COUPLE OF THEM OUT FIVE TIMES!

Grid 1

x	2	5	10
11			
6			
3			
9			
2			
12			
4			
5			
9			
12			
7			
8			
Time =		Total =	

Grid 1 Answers

x	2	5	10
11	22	55	66
6	12	30	60
3	6	15	30
9	18	45	90
2	4	10	20
12	24	60	120
4	8	20	40
5	10	25	50
9	18	45	90
12	24	60	120
7	14	35	70
8	16	40	80

Self Assessment

Star Rating

How successful was I with my times table grid?

Feeling

How do I feel about my results?

Tick one of the faces to show how you feel about your times tables.				
Key Objectives	🙁	😐	🙂	Parent/Child
2x table				
5x table				
10x table				
Speed				

Steps to becoming a **MASTER!**

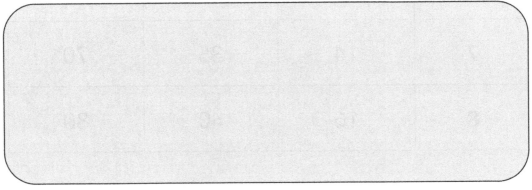

Grid 2

x	10	5	2
6			
2			
8			
4			
10			
5			
3			
7			
12			
9			
11			
1			
Time =		Total =	

Grid 2 Answers

x	10	5	2
6	60	30	12
2	20	10	4
8	80	40	16
4	40	20	8
10	100	50	20
5	50	25	10
3	30	15	6
7	70	35	14
12	120	60	24
9	90	45	18
11	110	55	22
1	10	5	2

Self Assessment

Star Rating

How successful was I with my times table grid?

Feeling

How do I feel about my results?

Tick one of the faces to show how you feel about your times tables.				
Key Objectives	☹	😐	😀	Parent/Child
2x table				
5x table				
10x table				
Speed				

Steps to becoming a __MASTER!__

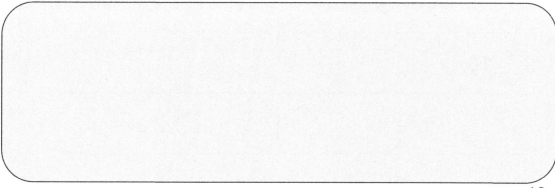

Grid 3

x	10	2	5
8			
6			
4			
11			
7			
9			
1			
3			
5			
12			
2			
10			
Time =		Total =	

Grid 3 Answers

x	10	2	5
8	80	16	40
6	60	12	30
4	40	8	20
11	110	22	55
7	70	14	35
9	90	18	45
1	10	2	5
3	30	6	15
5	50	10	25
12	120	24	60
2	20	4	10
10	100	20	50

Self Assessment

Star Rating

How successful was I with my times table grid?

Feeling

How do I feel about my results?

Tick one of the faces to show how you feel about your times tables.			
Key Objectives	🙁	😐	😀	Parent/Child
2x table				
5x table				
10x table				
Speed				

Steps to becoming a **MASTER!**

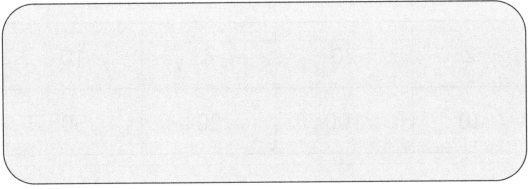

Grid 4

x	2	10	5
1			
12			
6			
8			
9			
11			
7			
4			
3			
2			
5			
10			
Time =		Total =	

Grid 4 Answers

x	2	10	5
1	2	10	5
12	24	120	60
6	12	60	30
8	16	80	40
9	18	90	45
11	22	110	55
7	14	70	35
4	8	40	20
3	6	30	15
2	4	20	10
5	10	50	25
10	20	100	50

Self Assessment

Star Rating

How successful was I with my times table grid?

Feeling

How do I feel about my results?

Tick one of the faces to show how you feel about your times tables.			
Key Objectives	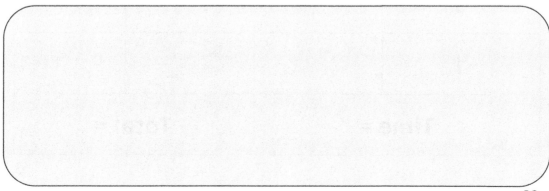		**Parent/Child**
2x table			
5x table			
10x table			
Speed			

Steps to becoming a <u>MASTER!</u>

Grid 5

x	5	2	10
6			
4			
9			
11			
7			
12			
2			
10			
8			
3			
5			
1			
Time =		Total =	

Grid 5 Answers

x	5	2	10
6	30	12	60
4	20	8	40
9	45	18	90
11	55	22	110
7	35	14	70
12	60	24	120
2	10	4	20
10	50	20	100
8	40	16	80
3	15	6	30
5	25	10	50
1	5	2	10

Self Assessment

Star Rating

How successful was I with my times table grid?

Feeling

How do I feel about my results?

Tick one of the faces to show how you feel about your times tables.				
Key Objectives	🙁	😐	🙂	**Parent/Child**
2x table				
5x table				
10x table				
Speed				

Steps to becoming a MASTER!

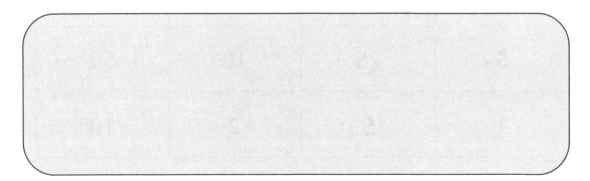

Grid 6

x	2	5	10
12			
3			
9			
1			
6			
11			
7			
4			
8			
5			
2			
10			
Time =		Total =	

26

Grid 6 Answers

x	2	5	10
12	24	60	120
3	6	15	30
9	18	45	90
1	2	5	10
6	12	30	60
11	22	55	110
7	14	35	70
4	8	20	40
8	16	40	80
5	10	25	50
2	4	10	20
10	20	50	100

Self Assessment

Star Rating

How successful was I with my times table grid?

Feeling

How do I feel about my results?

Tick one of the faces to show how you feel about your times tables.				
Key Objectives	🙁	😐	🙂	Parent/Child
2x table				
5x table				
10x table				
Speed				

Steps to becoming a <u>MASTER!</u>

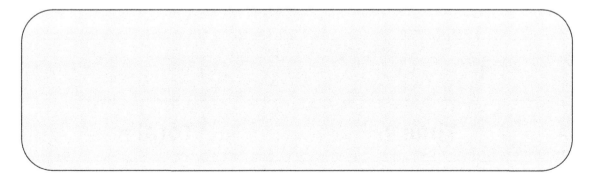

28

Grid 7

x	10	5	2
6			
9			
12			
2			
8			
11			
5			
4			
3			
7			
10			
1			
Time =		Total =	

Grid 7 Answers

x	10	5	2
6	60	30	12
9	90	45	18
12	120	60	24
2	20	10	4
8	80	40	16
11	110	55	22
5	50	25	10
4	40	20	8
3	30	15	6
7	70	35	14
10	100	50	20
1	10	5	2

Self Assessment

Star Rating

How successful was I with my times table grid?

Feeling

How do I feel about my results?

Tick one of the faces to show how you feel about your times tables.				
Key Objectives	☹	😐	😊	**Parent/Child**
2x table				
5x table				
10x table				
Speed				

Steps to becoming a <u>MASTER!</u>

Grid 8

x	2	5	10
6			
1			
3			
7			
4			
12			
11			
2			
9			
8			
5			
10			
Time =		Total =	

Grid 8 Answers

x	2	5	10
6	12	30	60
1	2	5	10
3	6	15	30
7	14	35	70
4	8	20	40
12	24	60	120
11	22	55	110
2	4	10	20
9	18	45	90
8	16	40	80
5	10	25	50
10	20	50	100

Self Assessment

Star Rating

How successful was I with my times table grid?

Feeling

How do I feel about my results?

Tick one of the faces to show how you feel about your times tables.				
Key Objectives	☹	😐	😊	Parent/Child
2x table				
5x table				
10x table				
Speed				

Steps to becoming a **MASTER!**

Grid 9

x	5	10	2
4			
8			
6			
3			
11			
9			
1			
2			
5			
7			
12			
10			
Time =		Total =	

Grid 9 Answers

x	5	10	2
4	20	40	8
8	40	80	16
6	30	60	12
3	15	30	6
11	55	110	22
9	45	90	18
1	5	10	2
2	10	20	4
5	25	50	10
7	35	70	14
12	60	120	24
10	50	100	20

Self Assessment

Star Rating

How successful was I with my times table grid?

Feeling

How do I feel about my results?

Tick one of the faces to show how you feel about your times tables.				
Key Objectives	🙁	😐	🙂	Parent/Child
2x table				
5x table				
10x table				
Speed				

Steps to becoming a **MASTER!**

Grid 10

x	10	2	5
4			
7			
2			
9			
6			
1			
12			
5			
8			
3			
11			
10			
Time =		Total =	

Grid 10 Answers

x	10	2	5
4	40	8	20
7	70	14	35
2	20	4	10
9	90	18	45
6	60	12	30
1	10	2	5
12	120	24	60
5	50	10	25
8	80	16	40
3	30	6	15
11	110	22	55
10	100	20	50

Self Assessment

Star Rating

How successful was I with my times table grid?

Feeling

How do I feel about my results?

Tick one of the faces to show how you feel about your times tables.				
Key Objectives	☹	😐	🙂	Parent/Child
2x table				
5x table				
10x table				
Speed				

Steps to becoming a MASTER!

Grid 11

x	2	5	10
8			
7			
6			
4			
3			
9			
1			
10			
12			
11			
5			
2			
Time =		Total =	

Grid 11 Answers

x	2	5	10
8	16	40	80
7	14	35	70
6	12	30	60
4	8	20	40
3	6	15	30
9	18	45	90
1	2	5	10
10	20	50	100
12	24	60	120
11	22	55	110
5	10	25	50
2	4	10	20

Self Assessment

Star Rating

How successful was I with my times table grid?

Feeling

How do I feel about my results?

Tick one of the faces to show how you feel about your times tables.				
Key Objectives	🙁	😐	😀	**Parent/Child**
2x table				
5x table				
10x table				
Speed				

Steps to becoming a <u>MASTER!</u>

Grid 12

x	5	10	2
3			
7			
2			
11			
9			
12			
1			
4			
6			
10			
8			
5			
Time =		Total =	

Grid 12 Answers

x	5	10	2
3	15	30	6
7	35	70	14
2	10	20	4
11	55	110	22
9	45	90	18
12	60	120	24
1	5	10	2
4	20	40	8
6	30	60	12
10	50	100	20
8	40	80	16
5	25	50	10

Self Assessment

Star Rating

How successful was I with my times table grid?

Feeling

How do I feel about my results?

Tick one of the faces to show how you feel about your times tables.				
Key Objectives	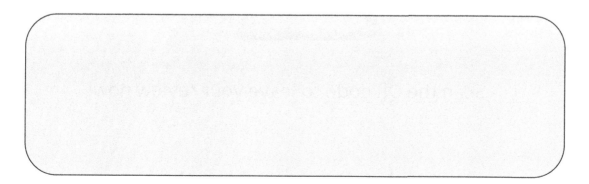			Parent/Child
2x table				
5x table				
10x table				
Speed				

Steps to becoming a **MASTER!**

REVIEW

Leave Your Mark with Sakura Learning!

Thank you for choosing our Super Times Tables Book! We're excited to be part of your child's journey to mastering times tables from 1-12. Scan the QR code below to leave a review and help other parents choose the best educational resources!

Your review matters! It guides parents, motivates our team, drives continuous improvement, and builds a supportive community. Together, let's empower children to excel in maths and love learning!

Scan the QR code to leave your review now!

MATHS MANIA

TIMES

TABLES

3, 6 AND 9X TABLES

Multiplication Mania!

Timed Tests for the 3x, 6x, and 9x Tables.

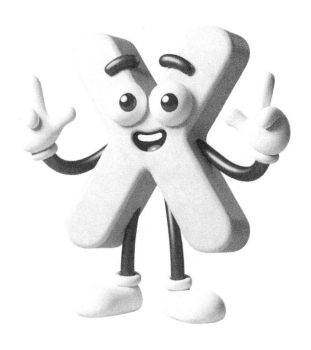

Introduction

Hey there, space cadet! 🚀 Ready to blast off into the universe of times tables? Each multiplication is like a magic key 🔑, unlocking the mysteries of maths in a cosmic treasure hunt!

Forget boring maths - times tables make it easy and fun! They're your shortcut to figuring out how many cupcakes 🧁 you can eat in a week. It's like adding, but at lightning speed!

The grids in this book? They're like a workout for your brain 🧠! You'll speed through numbers like a pro, repeating them like a catchy tune 🎵, and racing against time ⏱️ adds a whole new level of excitement!

With these grids as your trusty sidekick, you'll be a maths superhero in no time! And guess what? You get to be your own guide! Analyzing your victories and oopsies 🔍 is like being a detective on a maths mission. Mistakes aren't failures; they're just stepping stones to mastering maths.

So, buckle up and prepare for an intergalactic adventure through the world of numbers. It's time to awaken your inner maths wizard! ✦

Times Tables 1-12

1

1 × 1 = 1
1 × 2 = 2
1 × 3 = 3
1 × 4 = 4
1 × 5 = 5
1 × 6 = 6
1 × 7 = 7
1 × 8 = 8
1 × 9 = 9
1 × 10 = 10
1 × 11 = 11
1 × 12 = 12

2

2 × 1 = 2
2 × 2 = 4
2 × 3 = 6
2 × 4 = 8
2 × 5 = 10
2 × 6 = 12
2 × 7 = 14
2 × 8 = 16
2 × 9 = 18
2 × 10 = 20
2 × 11 = 22
2 × 12 = 24

3

3 × 1 = 3
3 × 2 = 6
3 × 3 = 9
3 × 4 = 12
3 × 5 = 15
3 × 6 = 18
3 × 7 = 21
3 × 8 = 24
3 × 9 = 27
3 × 10 = 30
3 × 11 = 33
3 × 12 = 36

4

4 × 1 = 4
4 × 2 = 8
4 × 3 = 12
4 × 4 = 16
4 × 5 = 20
4 × 6 = 24
4 × 7 = 28
4 × 8 = 32
4 × 9 = 36
4 × 10 = 40
4 × 11 = 44
4 × 12 = 48

5

5 × 1 = 5
5 × 2 = 10
5 × 3 = 15
5 × 4 = 20
5 × 5 = 25
5 × 6 = 30
5 × 7 = 35
5 × 8 = 40
5 × 9 = 45
5 × 10 = 50
5 × 11 = 55
5 × 12 = 60

6

6 × 1 = 6
6 × 2 = 12
6 × 3 = 18
6 × 4 = 24
6 × 5 = 30
6 × 6 = 36
6 × 7 = 42
6 × 8 = 48
6 × 9 = 54
6 × 10 = 60
6 × 11 = 66
6 × 12 = 72

7

7 × 1 = 7
7 × 2 = 14
7 × 3 = 21
7 × 4 = 28
7 × 5 = 35
7 × 6 = 42
7 × 7 = 49
7 × 8 = 56
7 × 9 = 63
7 × 10 = 70
7 × 11 = 77
7 × 12 = 84

8

8 × 1 = 8
8 × 2 = 16
8 × 3 = 24
8 × 4 = 32
8 × 5 = 40
8 × 6 = 48
8 × 7 = 56
8 × 8 = 64
8 × 9 = 72
8 × 10 = 80
8 × 11 = 88
8 × 12 = 96

9

9 × 1 = 9
9 × 2 = 18
9 × 3 = 27
9 × 4 = 36
9 × 5 = 45
9 × 6 = 54
9 × 7 = 63
9 × 8 = 72
9 × 9 = 81
9 × 10 = 90
9 × 11 = 99
9 × 12 = 108

10

10 × 1 = 10
10 × 2 = 20
10 × 3 = 30
10 × 4 = 40
10 × 5 = 50
10 × 6 = 60
10 × 7 = 70
10 × 8 = 80
10 × 9 = 90
10 × 10 = 100
10 × 11 = 110
10 × 12 = 120

11

11 × 1 = 11
11 × 2 = 22
11 × 3 = 33
11 × 4 = 44
11 × 5 = 55
11 × 6 = 66
11 × 7 = 77
11 × 8 = 88
11 × 9 = 99
11 × 10 = 110
11 × 11 = 121
11 × 12 = 132

12

12 × 1 = 12
12 × 2 = 24
12 × 3 = 36
12 × 4 = 48
12 × 5 = 60
12 × 6 = 72
12 × 7 = 84
12 × 8 = 96
12 × 9 = 108
12 × 10 = 120
12 × 11 = 132
12 × 12 = 144

3x Table

1 X 3 = 3

2 X 3 = 6

3 X 3 = 9

4 X 3 = 12

5 X 3 = 15

6 X 3 = 18

7 X 3 = 21

8 X 3 = 24

9 X 3 = 27

10 X 3 = 30

11 x 3 = 33

12 x 3 = 36

6x Table

1 X 6 = 6
2 X 6 = 12
3 X 6 = 18
4 X 6 = 24
5 X 6 = 30
6 X 6 = 36
7 X 6 = 42
8 X 6 = 48
9 X 6 = 54
10 X 6 = 60
11 x 6 = 66
12 x 6 = 72

9x Table

1 X 9 = 9
2 X 9 = 18
3 X 9 = 27
4 X 9 = 36
5 X 9 = 45
6 X 9 = 54
7 X 9 = 63
8 X 9 = 72
9 X 9 = 81
10 X 9 = 90
11 x 9 = 99
12 x 9 = 108

TIMES TABLES GRIDS

Instructions for the Grids

Are you ready for a thrilling maths adventure? We're about to master the 3, 6, and 9 times tables with a secret magic grid that holds the key to unlocking hidden treasures of knowledge! ✦

1 First, let's get your grid ready! Each row and column is a pathway leading to answers you seek.

2 Pick a number, find its corresponding row, then swoop down to meet another number's column. Are you ready to multiply? You're now a daring number explorer! 🔍

3 Did you find the spot where the row and column meet? Look no further, you've found a treasure! Write down that precious number.

4 It's time for some detective work! 🕵 Study your grid, high-five yourself for correct answers with a tick (✓), and mark areas for improvement with a burst of colour.

Are you ready to conquer those times tables? Let's dive in! Need help? Check out the answers at the back of this second book. But no peeking at other grids! 🙈 Let the maths adventure begin! 🚀

For a clear guide, flip to the next page to see a diagram with step-by-step instructions! Happy exploring!

HOW TO USE THE GRID

	Example		
x	3	6	9
1	3	6	9
2	6	12	18
3	9	18	27
4	12	24	36
5	15	30	45
6	18	36	54
7	21	42	63
8	24	48	72
9	27	54	82
10	30	60	90
11	33	66	99
12	36	74	108
Total	12	12	12
Time = 10mins 20secs		Total = 34	

SPOT THE SLIP-UP, SO YOU CAN PERFECT IT NEXT TIME.

CLOCK IN YOUR GRID COMPLETION TIME.

TALLY UP YOUR SCORE AND JOT IT DOWN!

INSTRUCTIONS FOR SELF-ASSESSING

Are you ready to become a maths wizard? Let's get cracking with some self-assessment, reflection, and goal-setting! 🚀 Use your trusty colouring pens ✏️ to fill in stars and happy faces, showing off your mad skills for each question. The more smiley faces, the more powerful you are! 😊

Tick off ✅ the times tables you've mastered and note down the ones that need a little more elbow grease 🔧. With a bit of help and some goal-setting magic, you'll be a pro in no time!

Don't fear the mistakes, embrace them with the Marvellous Mistake Mission! Pick three noteworthy errors and rewrite them five times. Focusing on your mistakes will help you turn them into wisdom! Feeling stuck? Set a new mini-goal to enhance your skills, like mastering the 5 times table. 🔮

By acknowledging your mistakes, practicing, and setting goals, you're already on your way to becoming a multiplication master! 🎩 ✨ Your colourful corrections and highlights will make your learning journey shine! ⭐ So, are you ready to take on this mathematical adventure? Let's go! 🌈

HOW TO USE SELF-ASSESSMENT

LET'S PAINT
THE STARS
WITH OUR
SUCCESS!

GIVE
YOURSELF A
FUN TICK ✅
TO SHOW
HOW YOU
FEEL AND
ADD A
COMMENT!

UNLEASH
YOUR
FEELINGS!
✦ TICK OR
COLOUR A
FACE TO
MATCH
YOUR
MOOD
ABOUT THE
RESULTS.
☺

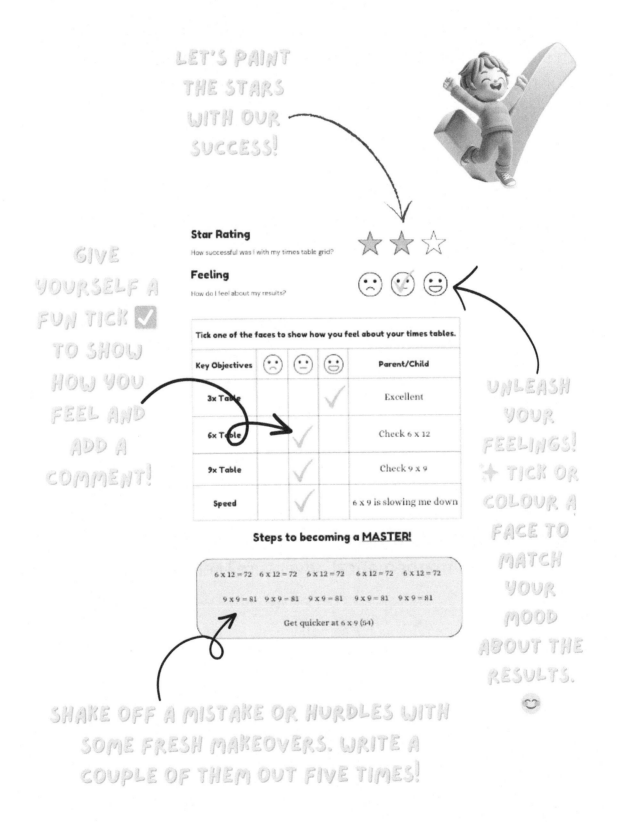

Star Rating

How successful was I with my times table grid?

Feeling

How do I feel about my results?

Tick one of the faces to show how you feel about your times tables.

Key Objectives	☹	😐	😃	Parent/Child
3x Table			✓	Excellent
6x Table		✓		Check 6 x 12
9x Table		✓		Check 9 x 9
Speed		✓		6 x 9 is slowing me down

Steps to becoming a **MASTER!**

6 x 12 = 72   6 x 12 = 72   6 x 12 = 72   6 x 12 = 72   6 x 12 = 72

9 x 9 = 81   9 x 9 = 81   9 x 9 = 81   9 x 9 = 81   9 x 9 = 81

Get quicker at 6 x 9 (54)

SHAKE OFF A MISTAKE OR HURDLES WITH
SOME FRESH MAKEOVERS. WRITE A
COUPLE OF THEM OUT FIVE TIMES!

Grid 1

x	3	6	9
11			
6			
3			
9			
2			
12			
4			
5			
9			
12			
7			
8			
Time =		Total =	

Grid 1 Answers

x	3	6	9
11	33	66	99
6	18	36	54
3	9	18	27
9	27	54	81
2	6	12	18
12	36	72	108
4	12	24	36
5	15	30	45
9	27	54	81
12	36	72	108
7	21	42	63
8	24	48	72

Self Assessment

Star Rating

How successful was I with my times table grid?

Feeling

How do I feel about my results?

Tick one of the faces to show how you feel about your times tables.				
Key Objectives	😞	😐	😊	Parent/Child
3x Table				
6x Table				
9x Table				
Speed				

Steps to becoming a **MASTER!**

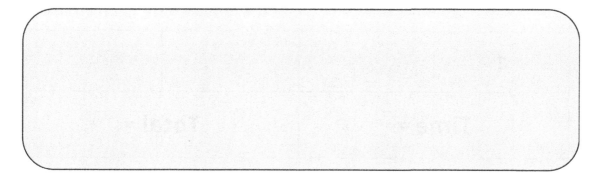

Grid 2

x	3	6	9
6			
2			
8			
4			
10			
5			
3			
7			
12			
9			
11			
1			
Time =		Total =	

Grid 2 Answers

x	3	6	9
6	18	36	54
2	6	12	18
8	24	48	72
4	12	24	36
10	30	60	90
5	15	30	45
3	9	18	27
7	21	42	63
12	36	72	108
9	27	54	81
11	33	66	99
1	3	6	9

Self Assessment

Star Rating

How successful was I with my times table grid?

Feeling

How do I feel about my results?

Tick one of the faces to show how you feel about your times tables.				
Key Objectives	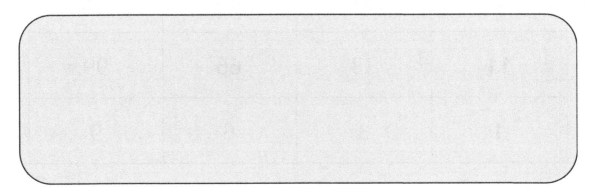			**Parent/Child**
3x Table				
6x Table				
9x Table				
Speed				

Steps to becoming a <u>MASTER!</u>

Grid 3

x	3	6	9
8			
6			
4			
11			
7			
9			
1			
3			
5			
12			
2			
10			
Time =		Total =	

Grid 3 Answers

x	3	6	9
8	24	48	72
6	18	36	54
4	12	24	36
11	33	66	99
7	21	42	63
9	27	54	81
1	3	6	9
3	9	18	27
5	15	30	45
12	36	72	108
2	6	12	18
10	30	60	90

Self Assessment

Star Rating

How successful was I with my times table grid?

Feeling

How do I feel about my results?

Tick one of the faces to show how you feel about your times tables.			
Key Objectives	😟	😐	😀	**Parent/Child**
3x Table				
6x Table				
9x Table				
Speed				

Steps to becoming a <u>MASTER!</u>

Grid 4

x	3	6	9
1			
12			
6			
8			
9			
11			
7			
4			
3			
2			
5			
10			
Time =		Total =	

Grid 4 Answers

x	3	6	9
1	3	6	9
12	36	72	108
6	18	36	54
8	24	48	72
9	27	54	81
11	33	66	99
7	21	42	63
4	12	24	36
3	9	18	27
2	6	12	18
5	15	30	45
10	30	60	90

Self Assessment

Star Rating

How successful was I with my times table grid?

Feeling

How do I feel about my results?

Tick one of the faces to show how you feel about your times tables.				
Key Objectives	😞	😐	😀	**Parent/Child**
3x Table				
6x Table				
9x Table				
Speed				

Steps to becoming a <u>MASTER!</u>

Grid 5

x	3	6	9
6			
4			
9			
11			
7			
12			
2			
10			
8			
3			
5			
1			
Time =		Total =	

Grid 5 Answers

x	3	6	9
6	18	36	54
4	12	24	36
9	27	54	81
11	33	66	99
7	21	42	63
12	36	72	108
2	6	12	18
10	30	60	90
8	24	48	72
3	9	18	27
5	15	30	45
1	3	6	9

Self Assessment

Star Rating

How successful was I with my times table grid?

Feeling

How do I feel about my results?

Tick one of the faces to show how you feel about your times tables.				
Key Objectives	☹	😐	🙂	**Parent/Child**
3x Table				
6x Table				
9x Table				
Speed				

Steps to becoming a <u>MASTER!</u>

Grid 6

x	3	6	9
12			
3			
9			
1			
6			
11			
7			
4			
8			
5			
2			
10			
Time =		Total =	

Grid 6 Answers

x	3	6	9
12	36	72	108
3	9	18	27
9	27	54	81
1	3	6	9
6	18	36	54
11	33	66	99
7	21	42	63
4	12	24	36
8	24	48	72
5	15	30	45
2	6	12	18
10	30	60	90

Self Assessment

Star Rating

How successful was I with my times table grid?

Feeling

How do I feel about my results?

Tick one of the faces to show how you feel about your times tables.				
Key Objectives	🙁	😐	🙂	**Parent/Child**
3x Table				
6x Table				
9x Table				
Speed				

Steps to becoming a <u>MASTER!</u>

Grid 7

x	3	6	9
6			
9			
12			
2			
8			
11			
5			
4			
3			
7			
10			
1			
Time =		Total =	

Grid 7 Answers

x	3	6	9
6	18	36	54
9	27	54	81
12	36	72	108
2	6	12	18
8	24	48	72
11	33	66	99
5	15	30	45
4	12	24	36
3	9	18	27
7	21	42	63
10	30	60	90
1	3	6	9

Self Assessment

Star Rating

How successful was I with my times table grid?

Feeling

How do I feel about my results?

Tick one of the faces to show how you feel about your times tables.				
Key Objectives	😦	😐	😀	Parent/Child
3x Table				
6x Table				
9x Table				
Speed				

Steps to becoming a **MASTER!**

Grid 8

x	3	6	9
6			
1			
3			
7			
4			
12			
11			
2			
9			
8			
5			
10			
Time =		Total =	

Grid 8 Answers

x	3	6	9
6	18	36	54
1	3	6	9
3	9	18	27
7	21	42	63
4	12	24	36
12	36	72	108
11	33	66	99
2	6	12	18
9	27	54	81
8	24	48	72
5	15	30	45
10	30	60	90

Self Assessment

Star Rating

How successful was I with my times table grid?

Feeling

How do I feel about my results?

Tick one of the faces to show how you feel about your times tables.				
Key Objectives	😟	😐	😀	Parent/Child
3x Table				
6x Table				
9x Table				
Speed				

Steps to becoming a <u>MASTER!</u>

Grid 9

x	3	6	9
4			
8			
6			
3			
11			
9			
1			
2			
5			
7			
12			
10			
Time =		Total =	

Grid 9 Answers

x	3	6	9
4	12	24	36
8	24	48	72
6	18	36	54
3	9	18	27
11	33	66	99
9	27	54	81
1	3	6	9
2	6	12	18
5	15	30	45
7	21	42	63
12	36	72	108
10	30	60	90

Self Assessment

Star Rating

How successful was I with my times table grid?

Feeling

How do I feel about my results?

Tick one of the faces to show how you feel about your times tables.				
Key Objectives	🙁	😐	🙂	**Parent/Child**
3x Table				
6x Table				
9x Table				
Speed				

Steps to becoming a <u>MASTER!</u>

Grid 10

x	3	6	9
4			
7			
2			
9			
6			
1			
12			
5			
8			
3			
11			
10			
Time =		Total =	

Grid 10 Answers

x	3	6	9
4	12	24	36
7	21	42	63
2	6	12	18
9	27	54	81
6	18	36	54
1	3	6	9
12	36	72	108
5	15	30	45
8	24	48	72
3	9	18	27
11	33	66	99
10	30	60	90

Self Assessment

Star Rating

How successful was I with my times table grid?

Feeling

How do I feel about my results?

Tick one of the faces to show how you feel about your times tables.				
Key Objectives	☹	😐	😊	Parent/Child
3x Table				
6x Table				
9x Table				
Speed				

Steps to becoming a <u>MASTER!</u>

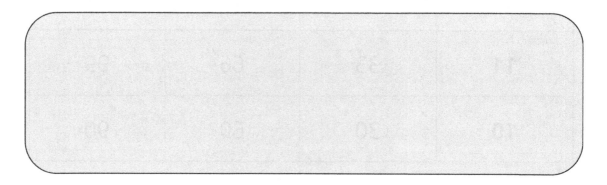

Grid 11

x	3	6	9
8			
7			
6			
4			
3			
9			
1			
10			
12			
11			
5			
2			
Time =		Total =	

Grid 11 Answers

x	3	6	9
8	24	48	72
7	21	42	63
6	18	36	54
4	12	24	36
3	9	18	27
9	27	54	81
1	3	6	9
10	30	60	90
12	36	72	108
11	33	66	99
5	15	30	45
2	6	12	18

Self Assessment

Star Rating

How successful was I with my times table grid?

Feeling

How do I feel about my results?

Tick one of the faces to show how you feel about your times tables.				
Key Objectives	☹	😐	😊	Parent/Child
3x Table				
6x Table				
9x Table				
Speed				

Steps to becoming a <u>MASTER!</u>

Grid 12

x	3	6	9
3			
7			
2			
11			
9			
12			
1			
4			
6			
10			
8			
5			
Time =		Total =	

Grid 12 Answers

x	3	6	9
3	9	18	27
7	21	42	63
2	6	12	18
11	33	66	99
9	27	54	81
12	36	72	108
1	3	6	9
4	12	24	36
6	18	36	54
10	30	60	90
8	24	48	72
5	15	30	45

Self Assessment

Star Rating

How successful was I with my times table grid?

Feeling

How do I feel about my results?

Tick one of the faces to show how you feel about your times tables.				
Key Objectives	🙁	😐	😃	**Parent/Child**
3x Table				
6x Table				
9x Table				
Speed				

Steps to becoming a <u>MASTER!</u>

REVIEW

 Leave Your Mark with Sakura Learning!

Thank you for choosing our Super Times Tables Book! We're excited to be part of your child's journey to mastering times tables from 1-12. Scan the QR code below to leave a review and help other parents choose the best educational resources!

Your review matters! It guides parents, motivates our team, drives continuous improvement, and builds a supportive community. Together, let's empower children to excel in maths and love learning!

Scan the QR code to leave your review now!

Super TIMES TABLES

4, 7 AND 8X TABLES
GROWTH MINDSET AND SELF ASSESSMENT

Multiplication Mania!

Timed Tests for the 4x, 7x and 8x Tables.

Introduction

Greetings, fellow adventurer! 🚀 Ready to embark on a mind-blowing journey through the amazing world of times tables? Think of each multiplication as a magical key 🔑, unlocking mysteries in a cosmic treasure hunt!

Times tables make maths a breeze, transforming it from a snooze-fest into a fun-filled adventure! It's your cheat code to figuring out how many donuts 🍩 you'll gobble in a month, or how many high-fives 🙌 you'll give in a year. It's like adding, but with turbo speed!

The grids in this book 📖 are like a gym for your brain 🧠, pumping you up to zoom through numbers like a pro. Practicing them is like learning an addictive tune 🎶, and racing against the clock ⏱ adds an extra thrill!

These grids will transform you into a maths superhero, and get this: You're the captain of your own journey! By analyzing your mistakes and victories, you become a detective 🔍 on a mission. Mistakes are merely stepping stones on your path to maths mastery.

So, buckle up for an epic ride through the universe of numbers, and unleash your inner maths wizard!

✦

Times Tables 1-12

1
1 × 1 = 1
1 × 2 = 2
1 × 3 = 3
1 × 4 = 4
1 × 5 = 5
1 × 6 = 6
1 × 7 = 7
1 × 8 = 8
1 × 9 = 9
1 × 10 = 10
1 × 11 = 11
1 × 12 = 12

2
2 × 1 = 2
2 × 2 = 4
2 × 3 = 6
2 × 4 = 8
2 × 5 = 10
2 × 6 = 12
2 × 7 = 14
2 × 8 = 16
2 × 9 = 18
2 × 10 = 20
2 × 11 = 22
2 × 12 = 24

3
3 × 1 = 3
3 × 2 = 6
3 × 3 = 9
3 × 4 = 12
3 × 5 = 15
3 × 6 = 18
3 × 7 = 21
3 × 8 = 24
3 × 9 = 27
3 × 10 = 30
3 × 11 = 33
3 × 12 = 36

4
4 × 1 = 4
4 × 2 = 8
4 × 3 = 12
4 × 4 = 16
4 × 5 = 20
4 × 6 = 24
4 × 7 = 28
4 × 8 = 32
4 × 9 = 36
4 × 10 = 40
4 × 11 = 44
4 × 12 = 48

5
5 × 1 = 5
5 × 2 = 10
5 × 3 = 15
5 × 4 = 20
5 × 5 = 25
5 × 6 = 30
5 × 7 = 35
5 × 8 = 40
5 × 9 = 45
5 × 10 = 50
5 × 11 = 55
5 × 12 = 60

6
6 × 1 = 6
6 × 2 = 12
6 × 3 = 18
6 × 4 = 24
6 × 5 = 30
6 × 6 = 36
6 × 7 = 42
6 × 8 = 48
6 × 9 = 54
6 × 10 = 60
6 × 11 = 66
6 × 12 = 72

7
7 × 1 = 7
7 × 2 = 14
7 × 3 = 21
7 × 4 = 28
7 × 5 = 35
7 × 6 = 42
7 × 7 = 49
7 × 8 = 56
7 × 9 = 63
7 × 10 = 70
7 × 11 = 77
7 × 12 = 84

8
8 × 1 = 8
8 × 2 = 16
8 × 3 = 24
8 × 4 = 32
8 × 5 = 40
8 × 6 = 48
8 × 7 = 56
8 × 8 = 64
8 × 9 = 72
8 × 10 = 80
8 × 11 = 88
8 × 12 = 96

9
9 × 1 = 9
9 × 2 = 18
9 × 3 = 27
9 × 4 = 36
9 × 5 = 45
9 × 6 = 54
9 × 7 = 63
9 × 8 = 72
9 × 9 = 81
9 × 10 = 90
9 × 11 = 99
9 × 12 = 108

10
10 × 1 = 10
10 × 2 = 20
10 × 3 = 30
10 × 4 = 40
10 × 5 = 50
10 × 6 = 60
10 × 7 = 70
10 × 8 = 80
10 × 9 = 90
10 × 10 = 100
10 × 11 = 110
10 × 12 = 120

11
11 × 1 = 11
11 × 2 = 22
11 × 3 = 33
11 × 4 = 44
11 × 5 = 55
11 × 6 = 66
11 × 7 = 77
11 × 8 = 88
11 × 9 = 99
11 x 10 = 110
11 x 11 = 121
11 x 12 = 132

12
12 × 1 = 12
12 × 2 = 24
12 × 3 = 36
12 × 4 = 48
12 × 5 = 60
12 × 6 = 72
12 × 7 = 84
12 × 8 = 96
12 × 9 = 108
12 × 10 = 120
12 × 11 = 132
12 × 12 = 144

4x Table

1 X 4 = 4

2 X 4 = 8

3 X 4 = 12

4 X 4 = 16

5 X 4 = 20

6 X 4 = 24

7 X 4 = 28

8 X 4 = 32

9 X 4 = 36

10 X 4 = 40

11 x 4 = 44

12 x 4 = 48

7x Table

1 X 7 = 7

2 X 7 = 14

3 X 7 = 21

4 X 7 = 28

5 X 7 = 35

6 X 7 = 42

7 X 7 = 49

8 X 7 = 56

9 X 7 = 63

10 X 7 = 70

11 x 7 = 77

12 x 7 = 84

8x Table

1 X 8 = 8

2 X 8 = 16

3 X 8 = 24

4 X 8 = 32

5 X 8 = 40

6 X 8 = 48

7 X 8 = 56

8 X 8 = 64

9 X 8 = 72

10 X 8 = 80

11 x 8 = 88

12 x 8 = 96

TIMES TABLES GRIDS

INSTRUCTIONS FOR THE GRIDS

Get ready for a math-tastic adventure! We're taking you on a magical journey through the 4, 7, and 8 times tables. Pack your bags and let's explore the hidden gems of multiplication! ✦

1️⃣ First things first, prepare your magic grid. Each row and column is a portal to the land of answers.

2️⃣ Choose a number and follow its row, then slide down to meet another number's column. Multiply! You're like Indiana Jones, but with numbers! 🔍

3️⃣ Have you found where the row and column meet? Congratulations! You've hit the jackpot! Jot down that precious number.

4️⃣ It's time to be a maths detective! 🕵 Analyze your grid, high-five yourself for correct answers (✔), and mark areas for improvement with a splash of colour.

Are you ready to take on these tables? Jump in and let's get started! Need help? The answers are in the back, but no cheating! 🙈 Let the maths adventure begin! 🚀

Flip to the next page for a step-by-step guide. Happy exploring!

HOW TO USE THE GRID

Example			
x	4	7	8
1	4	7	8
2	8	14	16
3	12	21	24
4	16	28	32
5	20	35	40
6	24	42	48
7	28	49	56
8	32	58	64
9	36	63	72
10	40	70	80
11	44	77	88
12	48	84	97
Total	12	12	12
Time = 10mins 20secs		Total = 34	

SPOT THE SLIP-UP, SO YOU CAN PERFECT IT NEXT TIME.

CLOCK IN YOUR GRID COMPLETION TIME.

TALLY UP YOUR SCORE AND JOT IT DOWN!

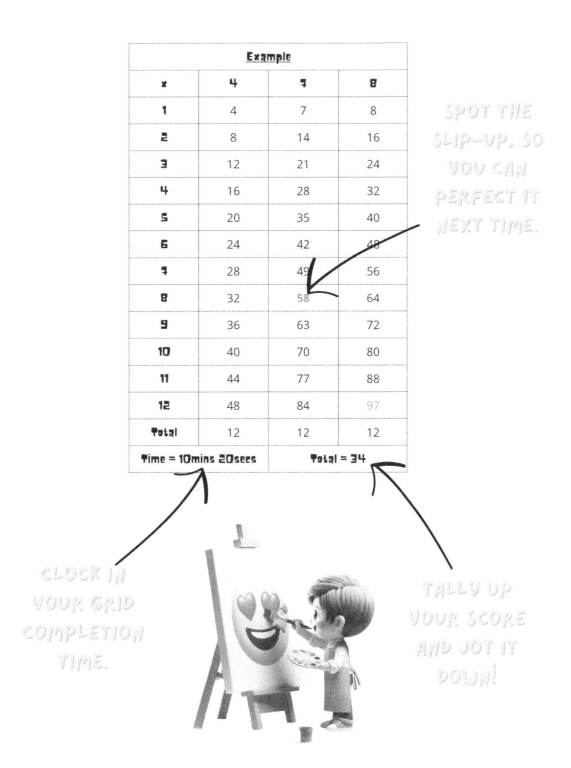

INSTRUCTIONS FOR SELF-ASSESSING

Let's get to the fun stuff - Self-Assessment, Reflection, and Goal-Setting! 🚀 Grab your favorite colouring pens 🖍 and let's light up some stars and faces! The more smiley faces, the more unstoppable you are! ☺

First, tick off ✅ the times tables you've conquered and give yourself a pat on the back. But don't forget to jot down the tricky ones 🔧. With a little extra help and some goal-setting magic, you'll be acing those too in no time!

Now, let's embrace the Marvellous Mistake Mission! Pick three of your most notable maths blunders and rewrite them five times each. Focusing on your mistakes is like a superpower that turns mishaps into wisdom! And if you get stuck, don't worry! Just set a new mini-goal, like mastering the 5 times table. You've got this! 🏃

By owning up to your mistakes, practicing, and setting goals, you're on your way to becoming a maths magician! 🎩✨ Your colourful corrections and highlights will make your learning journey glow! ⭐ Are you ready to take on the challenge and become a multiplication master? Let's go on this exciting adventure together! 🌈

HOW TO USE SELF-ASSESSMENT

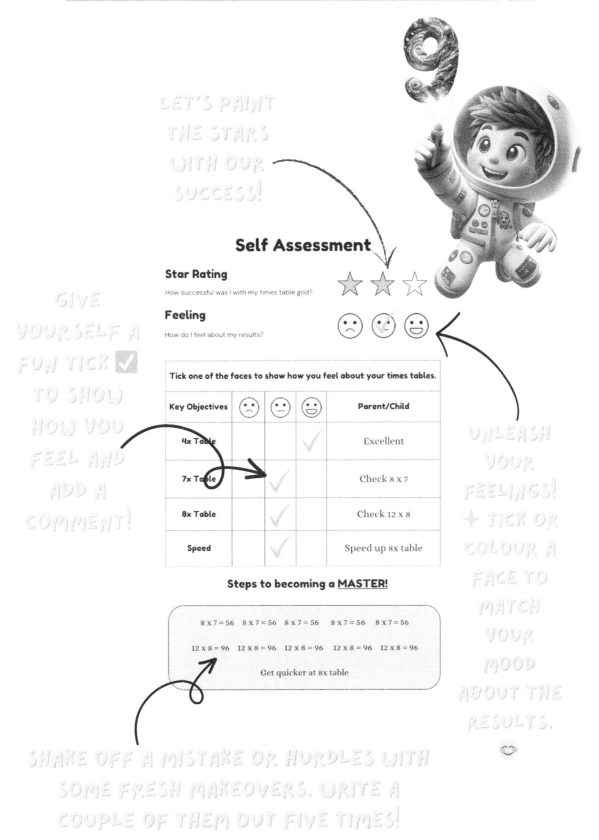

LET'S PAINT THE STARS WITH OUR SUCCESS!

GIVE YOURSELF A FUN TICK ✅ TO SHOW HOW YOU FEEL AND ADD A COMMENT!

UNLEASH YOUR FEELINGS! ✦ TICK OR COLOUR A FACE TO MATCH YOUR MOOD ABOUT THE RESULTS.

SHAKE OFF A MISTAKE OR HURDLES WITH SOME FRESH MAKEOVERS. WRITE A COUPLE OF THEM OUT FIVE TIMES!

Self Assessment

Star Rating

How successful was I with my times table grid?

Feeling

How do I feel about my results?

Tick one of the faces to show how you feel about your times tables.

Key Objectives	😦	😐	😃	Parent/Child
4x Table			✓	Excellent
7x Table		✓		Check 8 x 7
8x Table		✓		Check 12 x 8
Speed		✓		Speed up 8x table

Steps to becoming a **MASTER!**

8 X 7 = 56   8 X 7 = 56   8 X 7 = 56   8 X 7 = 56   8 X 7 = 56

12 X 8 = 96   12 X 8 = 96   12 X 8 = 96   12 X 8 = 96   12 X 8 = 96

Get quicker at 8x table

Grid 1

x	4	7	8
11			
6			
3			
9			
2			
12			
4			
5			
9			
12			
7			
8			
Time =		Total =	

Grid 1 Answers

x	4	7	8
11	44	77	88
6	24	42	48
3	12	21	24
9	36	63	72
2	8	14	16
12	48	84	96
4	16	28	32
5	20	35	40
9	36	63	72
12	48	84	96
7	28	49	56
8	32	56	64

Self Assessment

Star Rating

How successful was I with my times table grid?

Feeling

How do I feel about my results?

Tick one of the faces to show how you feel about your times tables.				
Key Objectives	😞	😐	😃	Parent/Child
4x Table				
7x Table				
8x Table				
Speed				

Steps to becoming a <u>MASTER!</u>

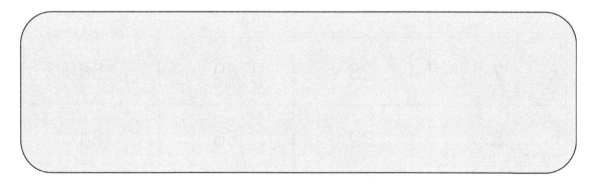

Grid 2

x	4	7	8
6			
2			
8			
4			
10			
5			
3			
7			
12			
9			
11			
1			
Time =		Total =	

Grid 2 Answers

x	4	7	8
6	24	42	48
2	8	14	16
8	32	56	64
4	16	28	32
10	40	70	80
5	20	35	40
3	12	21	24
7	28	49	56
12	48	84	96
9	36	63	72
11	44	77	88
1	4	7	8

Self Assessment

Star Rating

How successful was I with my times table grid?

Feeling

How do I feel about my results?

Tick one of the faces to show how you feel about your times tables.				
Key Objectives	☹	😐	😀	**Parent/Child**
4x Table				
7x Table				
8x Table				
Speed				

Steps to becoming a <u>MASTER!</u>

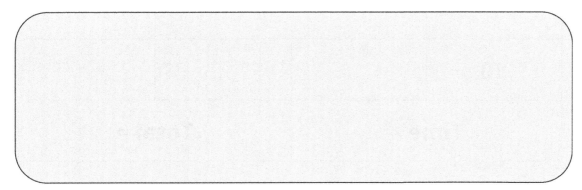

112

Grid 3

x	4	7	8
8			
6			
4			
11			
7			
9			
1			
3			
5			
12			
2			
10			
Time =		Total =	

Grid 3 Answers

x	4	7	8
8	32	56	64
6	24	42	48
4	16	28	32
11	44	77	88
7	28	49	56
9	36	63	72
1	4	7	8
3	12	21	24
5	20	35	40
12	48	84	96
2	8	14	16
10	40	70	80

Self Assessment

Star Rating

How successful was I with my times table grid?

Feeling

How do I feel about my results?

Tick one of the faces to show how you feel about your times tables.				
Key Objectives	🙁	😐	🙂	Parent/Child
4x Table				
7x Table				
8x Table				
Speed				

Steps to becoming a __MASTER!__

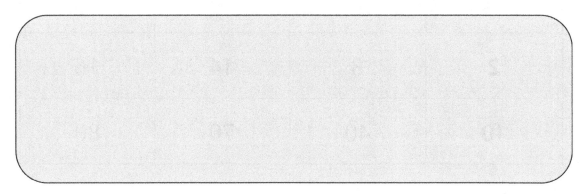

Grid 4

x	4	7	8
1			
12			
6			
8			
9			
11			
7			
4			
3			
2			
5			
10			
Time =		Total =	

Grid 4 Answers

x	4	7	8
1	4	7	8
12	48	84	96
6	24	42	48
8	32	56	64
9	36	63	72
11	44	77	88
7	28	49	56
4	16	28	32
3	12	21	24
2	8	14	16
5	20	35	40
10	40	70	80

Self Assessment

Star Rating

How successful was I with my times table grid?

Feeling

How do I feel about my results?

Tick one of the faces to show how you feel about your times tables.				
Key Objectives	☹	😐	🙂	Parent/Child
4x Table				
7x Table				
8x Table				
Speed				

Steps to becoming a MASTER!

Grid 5

x	4	7	8
6			
4			
9			
11			
7			
12			
2			
10			
8			
3			
5			
1			
Time =		Total =	

Grid 5 Answers

x	4	7	8
6	24	42	48
4	16	28	32
9	36	63	72
11	44	77	88
7	28	49	56
12	48	84	96
2	8	14	16
10	40	70	80
8	32	56	64
3	12	21	24
5	20	35	40
1	4	7	8

Self Assessment

Star Rating

How successful was I with my times table grid?

Feeling

How do I feel about my results?

Tick one of the faces to show how you feel about your times tables.				
Key Objectives	☹	😐	🙂	**Parent/Child**
4x Table				
7x Table				
8x Table				
Speed				

Steps to becoming a <u>MASTER!</u>

Grid 6

x	4	7	8
12			
3			
9			
1			
6			
11			
7			
4			
8			
5			
2			
10			
Time =		Total =	

Grid 6 Answers

x	4	7	8
12	48	84	96
3	12	21	24
9	36	63	72
1	4	7	8
6	24	42	48
11	44	77	88
7	28	49	56
4	16	28	32
8	32	56	64
5	20	35	40
2	8	14	16
10	40	70	80

Self Assessment

Star Rating

How successful was I with my times table grid?

Feeling

How do I feel about my results?

Tick one of the faces to show how you feel about your times tables.				
Key Objectives	😕	😐	😀	Parent/Child
4x Table				
7x Table				
8x Table				
Speed				

Steps to becoming a **MASTER!**

Grid 7

x	4	7	8
6			
9			
12			
2			
8			
11			
5			
4			
3			
7			
10			
1			
Time =		Total =	

Grid 7 Answers

x	4	7	8
6	24	42	48
9	36	63	72
12	48	84	96
2	8	14	16
8	32	56	64
11	44	77	88
5	20	35	40
4	16	28	32
3	12	21	24
7	28	49	56
10	40	70	80
1	4	7	8

Self Assessment

Star Rating

How successful was I with my times table grid?

Feeling

How do I feel about my results?

Tick one of the faces to show how you feel about your times tables.				
Key Objectives	🙁	😐	🙂	Parent/Child
4x Table				
7x Table				
8x Table				
Speed				

Steps to becoming a <u>MASTER!</u>

Grid 8

x	4	7	8
6			
1			
3			
7			
4			
12			
11			
2			
9			
8			
5			
10			
Time =		Total =	

Grid 8 Answers

x	4	7	8
6	24	42	48
1	4	7	8
3	12	21	24
7	28	49	56
4	16	28	32
12	48	84	96
11	44	77	88
2	8	14	16
9	36	63	72
8	32	56	64
5	20	35	40
10	40	70	80

Self Assessment

Star Rating

How successful was I with my times table grid?

Feeling

How do I feel about my results?

Tick one of the faces to show how you feel about your times tables.			
Key Objectives	🙁	😐	🙂	**Parent/Child**
4x Table				
7x Table				
8x Table				
Speed				

Steps to becoming a <u>MASTER!</u>

Grid 9

x	4	7	8
4			
8			
6			
3			
11			
9			
1			
2			
5			
7			
12			
10			
Time =		Total =	

Grid 9 Answers

x	4	7	8
4	16	28	32
8	32	56	64
6	24	42	48
3	12	21	24
11	44	77	88
9	36	63	72
1	4	7	8
2	8	14	16
5	20	35	40
7	28	49	56
12	48	84	96
10	40	70	80

Self Assessment

Star Rating

How successful was I with my times table grid?

Feeling

How do I feel about my results?

Tick one of the faces to show how you feel about your times tables.				
Key Objectives	😟	😐	😀	**Parent/Child**
4x Table				
7x Table				
8x Table				
Speed				

Steps to becoming a **MASTER!**

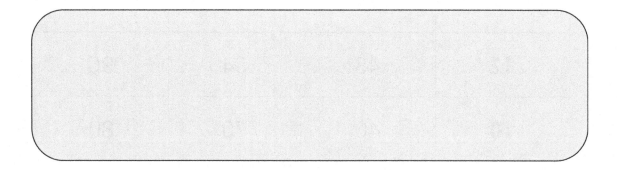

133

Grid 10

x	4	7	8
4			
7			
2			
9			
6			
1			
12			
5			
8			
3			
11			
10			
Time =		Total =	

Grid 10 Answers

x	4	7	8
4	16	28	32
7	28	49	56
2	8	14	16
9	36	63	72
6	24	42	48
1	4	7	8
12	48	84	96
5	20	35	40
8	32	56	64
3	12	21	24
11	44	77	88
10	40	70	80

Self Assessment

Star Rating

How successful was I with my times table grid?

Feeling

How do I feel about my results?

Tick one of the faces to show how you feel about your times tables.				
Key Objectives	☹	😐	☺	Parent/Child
4x Table				
7x Table				
8x Table				
Speed				

Steps to becoming a __MASTER!__

Grid 11

x	4	7	8
8			
7			
6			
4			
3			
9			
1			
10			
12			
11			
5			
2			
Time =		Total =	

Grid 11 Answers

x	4	7	8
8	32	56	64
7	28	49	56
6	24	42	48
4	16	28	32
3	12	21	24
9	36	63	72
1	4	7	8
10	40	70	80
12	48	84	96
11	44	77	88
5	20	35	40
2	8	14	16

Self Assessment

Star Rating

How successful was I with my times table grid?

Feeling

How do I feel about my results?

Tick one of the faces to show how you feel about your times tables.				
Key Objectives	😟	😐	😀	**Parent/Child**
4x Table				
7x Table				
8x Table				
Speed				

Steps to becoming a <u>MASTER!</u>

Grid 12

x	4	7	8
3			
7			
2			
11			
9			
12			
1			
4			
6			
10			
8			
5			
Time =		Total =	

Grid 12 Answers

x	4	7	8
3	12	21	24
7	28	49	56
2	8	14	16
11	44	77	88
9	36	63	72
12	48	84	96
1	4	7	8
4	16	28	32
6	24	42	48
10	40	70	80
8	32	56	64
5	20	35	40

Self Assessment

Star Rating

How successful was I with my times table grid?

Feeling

How do I feel about my results?

Tick one of the faces to show how you feel about your times tables.				
Key Objectives	🙁	😐	🙂	Parent/Child
4x Table				
7x Table				
8x Table				
Speed				

Steps to becoming a **MASTER!**

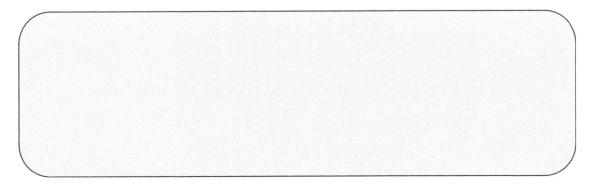

REVIEW

Leave Your Mark with Sakura Learning!

Thank you for choosing our Super Times Tables Book! We're excited to be part of your child's journey to mastering times tables from 1-12. Scan the QR code below to leave a review and help other parents choose the best educational resources!

Your review matters! It guides parents, motivates our team, drives continuous improvement, and builds a supportive community. Together, let's empower children to excel in maths and love learning!

Scan the QR code to leave your review now!

Multiplication Mania!

Timed Tests for the 11x and 12x Tables.

Introduction

Hey there! Let's dive into the magic of times tables for the 11 and 12 times tables!

Times tables are like the secret keys to maths. They make maths more fun and help you unlock doors to exciting adventures.

When we multiply numbers, it's like adding the same number multiple times. Times tables show us these quick shortcuts, like knowing how many candies you'll have if you get 4 candies every day for a week!

The grids in this book are like brain-training games! Practice with them, and you'll become a times table superhero for the 11 and 12 times tables.
It's like racing against the clock, challenging yourself to fill in the answers as fast as lightning!

Remember, mistakes are stepping stones to getting better, just like learning new things.

So, become a maths superstar with this book, and embark on a journey to maths greatness for the 11 and 12 times tables! "

Times Tables 1-12

1

1 × 1 = 1
1 × 2 = 2
1 × 3 = 3
1 × 4 = 4
1 × 5 = 5
1 × 6 = 6
1 × 7 = 7
1 × 8 = 8
1 × 9 = 9
1 × 10 = 10
1 × 11 = 11
1 × 12 = 12

2

2 × 1 = 2
2 × 2 = 4
2 × 3 = 6
2 × 4 = 8
2 × 5 = 10
2 × 6 = 12
2 × 7 = 14
2 × 8 = 16
2 × 9 = 18
2 × 10 = 20
2 × 11 = 22
2 × 12 = 24

3

3 × 1 = 3
3 × 2 = 6
3 × 3 = 9
3 × 4 = 12
3 × 5 = 15
3 × 6 = 18
3 × 7 = 21
3 × 8 = 24
3 × 9 = 27
3 × 10 = 30
3 × 11 = 33
3 × 12 = 36

4

4 × 1 = 4
4 × 2 = 8
4 × 3 = 12
4 × 4 = 16
4 × 5 = 20
4 × 6 = 24
4 × 7 = 28
4 × 8 = 32
4 × 9 = 36
4 × 10 = 40
4 × 11 = 44
4 × 12 = 48

5

5 × 1 = 5
5 × 2 = 10
5 × 3 = 15
5 × 4 = 20
5 × 5 = 25
5 × 6 = 30
5 × 7 = 35
5 × 8 = 40
5 × 9 = 45
5 × 10 = 50
5 × 11 = 55
5 × 12 = 60

6

6 × 1 = 6
6 × 2 = 12
6 × 3 = 18
6 × 4 = 24
6 × 5 = 30
6 × 6 = 36
6 × 7 = 42
6 × 8 = 48
6 × 9 = 54
6 × 10 = 60
6 × 11 = 66
6 × 12 = 72

7

7 × 1 = 7
7 × 2 = 14
7 × 3 = 21
7 × 4 = 28
7 × 5 = 35
7 × 6 = 42
7 × 7 = 49
7 × 8 = 56
7 × 9 = 63
7 × 10 = 70
7 × 11 = 77
7 × 12 = 84

8

8 × 1 = 8
8 × 2 = 16
8 × 3 = 24
8 × 4 = 32
8 × 5 = 40
8 × 6 = 48
8 × 7 = 56
8 × 8 = 64
8 × 9 = 72
8 × 10 = 80
8 × 11 = 88
8 × 12 = 96

9

9 × 1 = 9
9 × 2 = 18
9 × 3 = 27
9 × 4 = 36
9 × 5 = 45
9 × 6 = 54
9 × 7 = 63
9 × 8 = 72
9 × 9 = 81
9 × 10 = 90
9 × 11 = 99
9 × 12 = 108

10

10 × 1 = 10
10 × 2 = 20
10 × 3 = 30
10 × 4 = 40
10 × 5 = 50
10 × 6 = 60
10 × 7 = 70
10 × 8 = 80
10 × 9 = 90
10 × 10 = 100
10 × 11 = 110
10 × 12 = 120

11

11 × 1 = 11
11 × 2 = 22
11 × 3 = 33
11 × 4 = 44
11 × 5 = 55
11 × 6 = 66
11 × 7 = 77
11 × 8 = 88
11 × 9 = 99
11 x 10 = 110
11 × 11 = 121
11 x 12 = 132

12

12 × 1 = 12
12 × 2 = 24
12 × 3 = 36
12 × 4 = 48
12 × 5 = 60
12 × 6 = 72
12 × 7 = 84
12 × 8 = 96
12 × 9 = 108
12 × 10 = 120
12 × 11 = 132
12 × 12 = 144

Warm up

x	2	3	4	5	6	7	8	9	10	11	12
2											
3											
4											
5											
6											
7											
8											
9											
10											
11											
12											
Total											

Time =   Total =

Warm-up Answers

x	2	3	4	5	6	7	8	9	10	11	12
2	4	6	8	10	12	14	16	18	20	22	24
3	6	9	12	15	18	21	24	27	30	33	36
4	8	12	16	20	24	28	32	36	40	44	48
5	10	15	20	25	30	35	40	45	50	55	60
6	12	18	24	30	36	42	48	54	60	66	72
7	14	21	28	35	42	49	56	63	70	77	84
8	16	24	32	40	48	56	64	72	80	88	96
9	18	27	36	45	54	63	72	81	90	99	108
10	20	30	40	50	60	70	80	90	100	110	120
11	22	33	44	55	66	77	88	99	110	121	132
12	24	36	48	60	72	84	96	108	120	132	144

11x Table

1 X 11 = 11
2 X 11 = 22
3 X 11 = 33
4 X 11 = 44
5 X 11 = 55
6 X 11 = 66
7 X 11 = 77
8 X 11 = 88
9 X 11 = 99
10 X 11 = 110
11 x 11 = 121
12 x 11 = 132

12x Table

1 X 12 = 12

2 X 12 = 24

3 X 12 = 36

4 X 12 = 48

5 X 12 = 60

6 X 12 = 72

7 X 12 = 84

8 X 12 = 96

9 X 12 = 108

10 X 12 = 120

11 x 12 = 132

12 x 12 = 144

TIMES TABLES GRIDS

INSTRUCTIONS FOR SELF-ASSESSING

Let's dive into this thrilling maths journey with the mighty 11 and 12 times tables! 🚀

Imagine your grid as a treasure map unveiling the secrets of the 11 and 12 times tables. Each row and column is a pathway to hidden answers. 📖

Check out the row with your chosen number and combine it with the column with another number. Multiply them together like a fearless number explorer! 🔍

Where the row and column intersect, you've unveiled a secret answer! Jot it down in the box, just like discovering buried treasure. 💲

Time to see how well you've cracked the multiplication mystery! Go through your magic grid and mark each answer with a triumphant checkmark (✓). If you need some help or want to verify your work, guess what? You can find the grid's answers at the back of your book! But remember, only peek at your own grid – no sneaky looks at the others!

And here's a pro tip: if you spot any answers that need a little touch-up, use a different colour to highlight them. It's like making them stand out, making corrections a breeze. 🎨✨🔢"

HOW TO USE SELF-ASSESSMENT

WE'RE GOING TO ROCK THIS PLANET WITH OUR TRIUMPH!

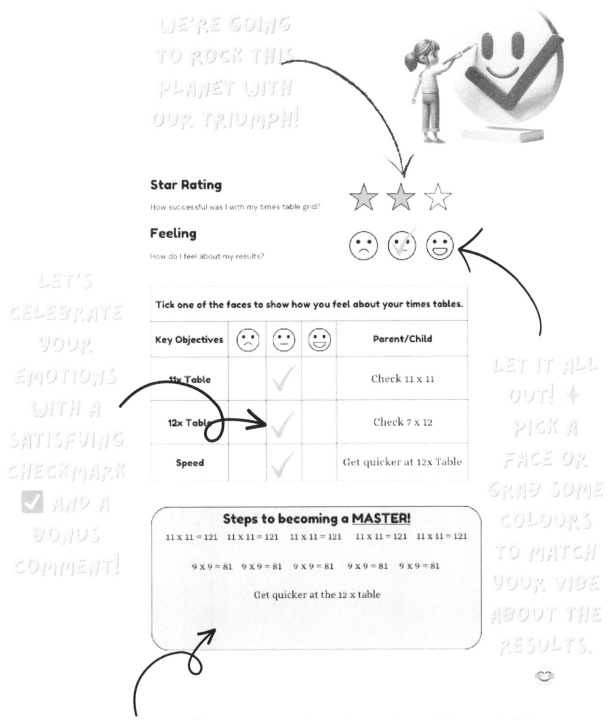

Star Rating

How successful was I with my times table grid?

Feeling

How do I feel about my results?

LET'S CELEBRATE YOUR EMOTIONS WITH A SATISFYING CHECKMARK ✅ AND A BONUS COMMENT!

LET IT ALL OUT! ✦ PICK A FACE OR GRAB SOME COLOURS TO MATCH YOUR VIBE ABOUT THE RESULTS. 💋

Tick one of the faces to show how you feel about your times tables.				
Key Objectives	☹	😐	😊	**Parent/Child**
11x Table		✓		Check 11 x 11
12x Table		✓		Check 7 x 12
Speed		✓		Get quicker at 12x Table

Steps to becoming a <u>MASTER!</u>

11 x 11 = 121   11 x 11 = 121   11 x 11 = 121   11 x 11 = 121   11 x 11 = 121

9 x 9 = 81   9 x 9 = 81   9 x 9 = 81   9 x 9 = 81   9 x 9 = 81

Get quicker at the 12 x table

BOUNCE BACK FROM MISSTEPS OR OBSTACLES WITH A SPRINKLE OF RENEWAL. PEN A FEW EXAMPLES, REPEATING THEM FIVEFOLD!

Grid 1

x	11	12
5		
2		
9		
3		
1		
10		
7		
12		
6		
8		
4		
11		
Time =		Total =

Grid 1 Answers

x	11	12
5	55	60
2	22	24
9	99	108
3	33	36
1	11	12
10	110	120
7	77	84
12	132	144
6	66	72
8	88	96
4	44	48
11	121	132

Self Assessment

Star Rating

How successful was I with my times table grid?

Feeling

How do I feel about my results?

Tick one of the faces to show how you feel about your times tables.				
Key Objectives	🙁	😐	🙂	Parent/Child
11x Table				
12x Table				
Speed				

Steps to becoming a <u>MASTER!</u>

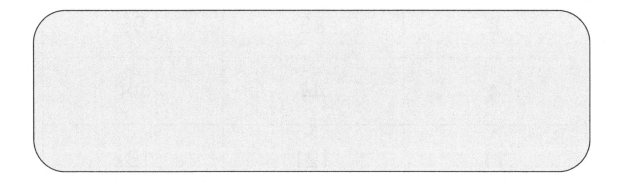

Grid 2

x	11	12
6		
1		
9		
5		
4		
8		
10		
3		
2		
7		
12		
11		
Time =		Total =

Grid 2 Answers

x	11	12
6	66	72
1	11	12
9	99	108
5	55	60
4	44	48
8	88	96
10	110	120
3	33	36
2	22	24
7	77	84
12	132	144
11	121	132

Self Assessment

Star Rating

How successful was I with my times table grid?

Feeling

How do I feel about my results?

Tick one of the faces to show how you feel about your times tables.				
Key Objectives	☹	😐	🙂	**Parent/Child**
11x Table				
12x Table				
Speed				

Steps to becoming a <u>MASTER!</u>

Grid 3

x	12	11
6		
1		
9		
2		
10		
3		
7		
8		
5		
4		
11		
12		
Time =		Total =

Grid 3 Answers

x	12	11
6	72	66
1	12	11
9	108	99
2	24	22
10	120	110
3	36	33
7	84	77
8	96	88
5	60	55
4	48	44
11	132	121
12	144	132

Self Assessment

Star Rating

How successful was I with my times table grid?

Feeling

How do I feel about my results?

Tick one of the faces to show how you feel about your times tables.				
Key Objectives	😟	😐	😀	**Parent/Child**
11x Table				
12x Table				
Speed				

Steps to becoming a <u>MASTER!</u>

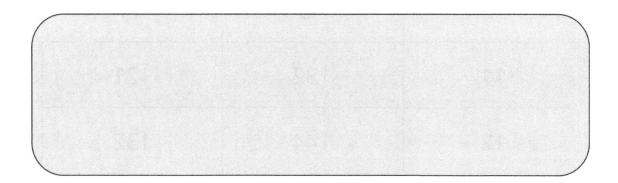

162

Grid 4

x	12	11
4		
9		
1		
5		
7		
3		
10		
8		
6		
2		
12		
11		
Time =		Total =

Grid 4 Answers

x	12	11
4	48	44
9	108	99
1	12	11
5	60	55
7	84	77
3	36	33
10	120	110
8	96	88
6	72	66
2	24	22
12	144	132
11	132	121

Self Assessment

Star Rating

How successful was I with my times table grid?

Feeling

How do I feel about my results?

Tick one of the faces to show how you feel about your times tables.				
Key Objectives	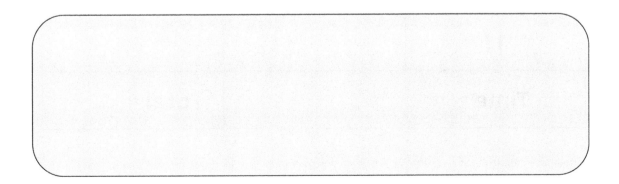			Parent/Child
11x Table				
12x Table				
Speed				

Steps to becoming a <u>MASTER!</u>

Grid 5

x	11	12
2		
6		
8		
4		
9		
1		
12		
3		
5		
7		
10		
11		
Time =	Total =	

Grid 5 Answers

x	11	12
2	22	24
6	66	72
8	88	96
4	44	48
9	99	108
1	11	12
12	132	144
3	33	36
5	55	60
7	77	84
10	110	120
11	121	132

Self Assessment

Star Rating

How successful was I with my times table grid?

Feeling

How do I feel about my results?

Tick one of the faces to show how you feel about your times tables.				
Key Objectives	🙁	😐	😀	**Parent/Child**
11x Table				
12x Table				
Speed				

Steps to becoming a **MASTER!**

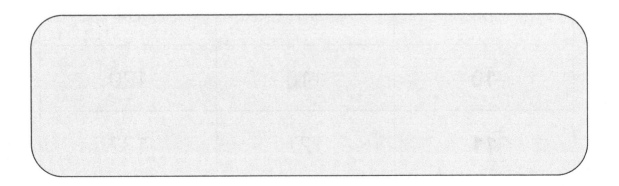

Grid 6

x	11	12
7		
3		
9		
6		
12		
1		
10		
4		
5		
2		
11		
8		
Time =	Total =	

Grid 6 Answers

x	11	12
7	77	84
3	33	36
9	99	108
6	66	72
12	132	144
1	11	12
10	110	120
4	44	48
5	55	60
2	22	24
11	121	132
8	88	96

Self Assessment

Star Rating

How successful was I with my times table grid?

Feeling

How do I feel about my results?

Tick one of the faces to show how you feel about your times tables.				
Key Objectives	☹	😐	🙂	**Parent/Child**
11x Table				
12x Table				
Speed				

Steps to becoming a <u>MASTER!</u>

Grid 7

x	12	11
5		
8		
3		
2		
10		
1		
6		
9		
7		
4		
12		
11		
Time =	Total =	

Grid 7 Answers

x	12	11
5	60	55
8	96	88
3	36	33
2	24	22
10	120	110
1	12	11
6	72	66
9	108	99
7	84	77
4	48	44
12	144	132
11	132	121

Self Assessment

Star Rating

How successful was I with my times table grid?

Feeling

How do I feel about my results?

Tick one of the faces to show how you feel about your times tables.				
Key Objectives	🙁	😐	🙂	Parent/Child
11x Table				
12x Table				
Speed				

Steps to becoming a <u>MASTER!</u>

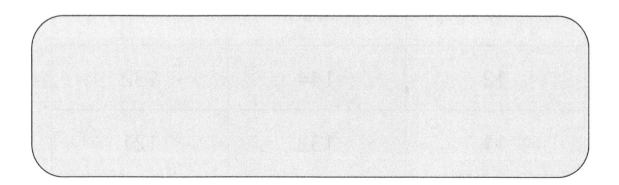

Grid 8

x	12	11
3		
6		
7		
8		
11		
4		
9		
5		
10		
12		
2		
1		
Time =		Total =

Grid 8 Answers

x	12	11
3	36	33
6	72	66
7	84	77
8	96	88
11	132	121
4	48	44
9	108	99
5	60	55
10	120	110
12	144	132
2	24	22
1	12	11

Self Assessment

Star Rating

How successful was I with my times table grid?

Feeling

How do I feel about my results?

Tick one of the faces to show how you feel about your times tables.				
Key Objectives	🙁	😐	🙂	Parent/Child
11x Table				
12x Table				
Speed				

Steps to becoming a <u>MASTER!</u>

Grid 9

x	11	12
5		
8		
2		
6		
12		
3		
10		
9		
4		
1		
11		
7		
Time =	Total =	

Grid 9 Answers

x	11	12
5	55	60
8	88	96
2	22	24
6	66	72
12	132	144
3	33	36
10	110	120
9	99	108
4	44	48
1	11	12
11	121	132
7	77	84

Self Assessment

Star Rating

How successful was I with my times table grid?

Feeling

How do I feel about my results?

Tick one of the faces to show how you feel about your times tables.				
Key Objectives	😦	😐	😃	Parent/Child
11x Table				
12x Table				
Speed				

Steps to becoming a MASTER!

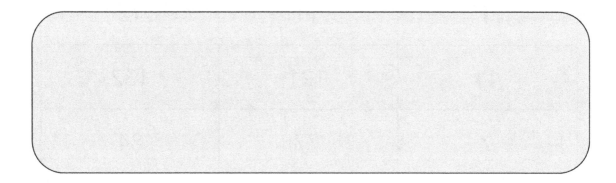

Grid 10

x	12	11
6		
9		
3		
8		
2		
10		
4		
7		
11		
5		
1		
12		
Time =		Total =

Grid 10 Answers

x	12	11
6	72	66
9	108	99
3	36	33
8	96	88
2	24	22
10	120	110
4	48	44
7	84	77
11	132	121
5	60	55
1	12	11
12	144	132

Self Assessment

Star Rating

How successful was I with my times table grid?

Feeling

How do I feel about my results?

Tick one of the faces to show how you feel about your times tables.			
Key Objectives	☹	😐	🙂	**Parent/Child**
11x Table				
12x Table				
Speed				

Steps to becoming a <u>MASTER!</u>

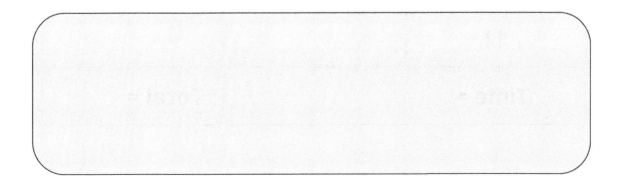

Grid 11

x	11	12
3		
8		
5		
2		
1		
10		
4		
6		
9		
12		
7		
11		
Time =	Total =	

Grid 11 Answers

x	11	12
3	33	36
8	88	96
5	55	60
2	22	24
1	11	12
10	110	120
4	44	48
6	66	72
9	99	108
12	132	144
7	77	84
11	121	132

Self Assessment

Star Rating

How successful was I with my times table grid?

Feeling

How do I feel about my results?

Tick one of the faces to show how you feel about your times tables.				
Key Objectives	🙁	😐	🙂	Parent/Child
11x Table				
12x Table				
Speed				

Steps to becoming a **MASTER!**

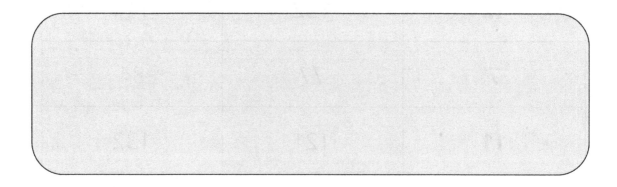

Grid 12

x	11	12
4		
8		
7		
1		
9		
5		
10		
3		
2		
6		
12		
11		
Time =	Total =	

Grid 12 Answers

x	11	12
4	44	48
8	88	96
7	77	84
1	11	12
9	99	108
5	55	60
10	110	120
3	33	36
2	22	24
6	66	72
12	132	144
11	121	132

Self Assessment

Star Rating

How successful was I with my times table grid?

Feeling

How do I feel about my results?

Tick one of the faces to show how you feel about your times tables.			
Key Objectives	☹	😐	😀	Parent/Child
11x Table				
12x Table				
Speed				

Steps to becoming a __MASTER!__

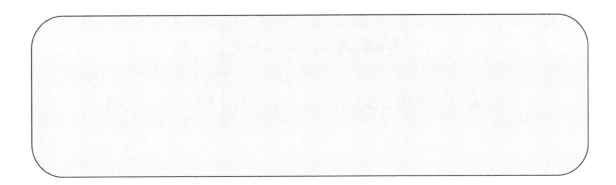

REVIEW

 Leave Your Mark with Sakura Learning!

Thank you for choosing our Super Times Tables Book! We're excited to be part of your child's journey to mastering times tables from 1-12. Scan the QR code below to leave a review and help other parents choose the best educational resources!

Your review matters! It guides parents, motivates our team, drives continuous improvement, and builds a supportive community. Together, let's empower children to excel in maths and love learning!

Scan the QR code to leave your review now!

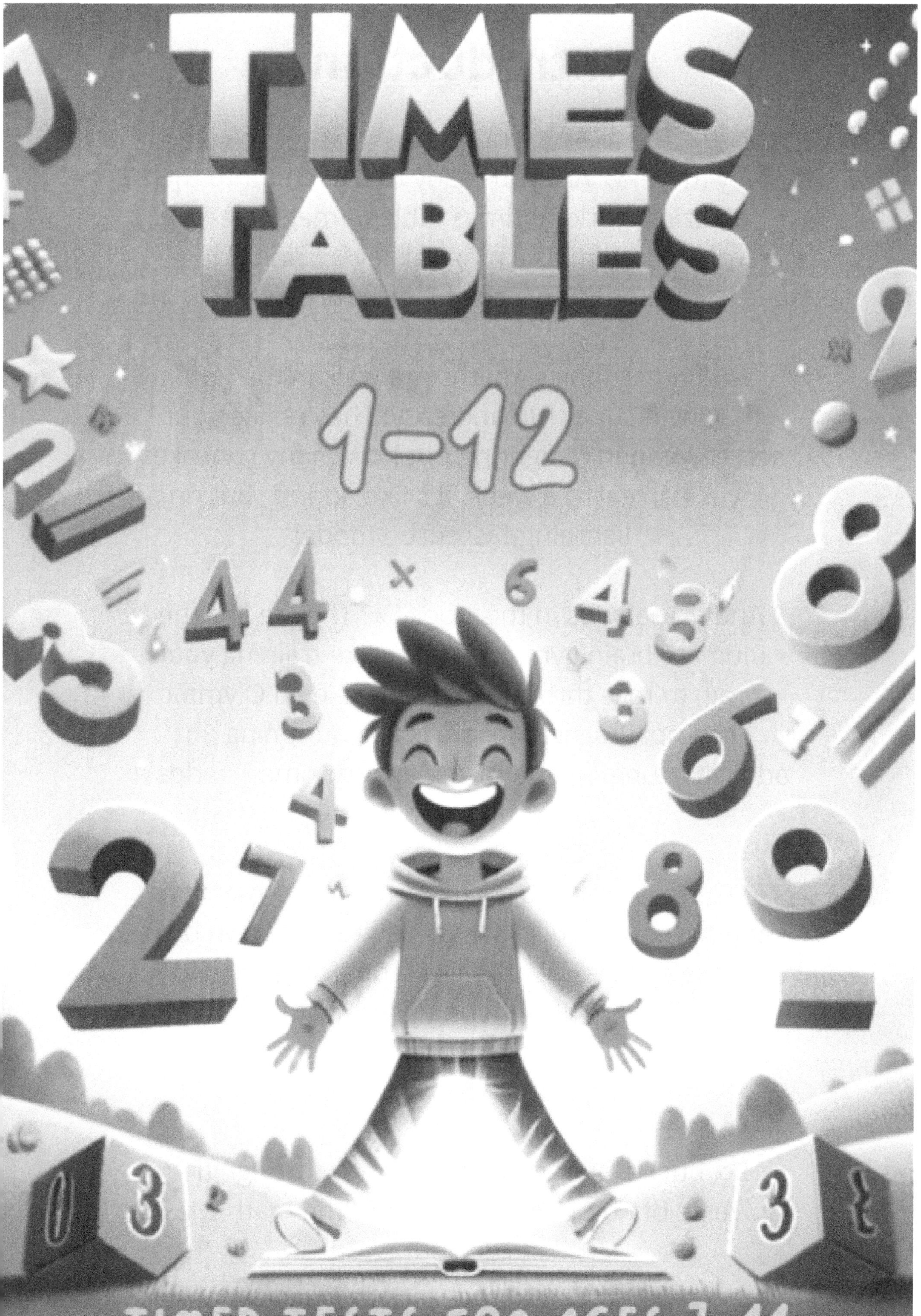
TIMES
TABLES
1-12
TIMED TESTS FOR AGES 7-11

Introduction

Hey there! 🚀 Are you ready to blast off into the amazing world of times tables? Imagine each multiplication as a magical key 🔑, unlocking mysteries on a cosmic treasure hunt!

With times tables, maths is a walk in the park, making it super fun and easy! They're like your secret weapon to figuring out how many cupcakes 🧁 you can eat in a week. It's like adding, but on a lightning-fast turbo mode!

And those grids in this book 📖? They're like the ultimate brain gym 🧠! They're like training your brain to race through numbers like an Olympic champ. Practicing them is like humming an addictive tune 🎶, and racing against time ⏱️ adds a thrill to it all!

These grids will transform you into a maths superhero. And guess what? You're your own boss! Your 'self-assessment' is like a detective's 🔍 work; it's all about deciphering your mistakes and victories. Mistakes aren't failures; they're just the stepping stones to mastering maths.

So, buckle up for an epic journey through the universe of numbers, and explore the math wizard inside you! ✦

Times Tables 1-12

1

1 × 1 = 1
1 × 2 = 2
1 × 3 = 3
1 × 4 = 4
1 × 5 = 5
1 × 6 = 6
1 × 7 = 7
1 × 8 = 8
1 × 9 = 9
1 × 10 = 10
1 × 11 = 11
1 × 12 = 12

2

2 × 1 = 2
2 × 2 = 4
2 × 3 = 6
2 × 4 = 8
2 × 5 = 10
2 × 6 = 12
2 × 7 = 14
2 × 8 = 16
2 × 9 = 18
2 × 10 = 20
2 × 11 = 22
2 × 12 = 24

3

3 × 1 = 3
3 × 2 = 6
3 × 3 = 9
3 × 4 = 12
3 × 5 = 15
3 × 6 = 18
3 × 7 = 21
3 × 8 = 24
3 × 9 = 27
3 × 10 = 30
3 × 11 = 33
3 × 12 = 36

4

4 × 1 = 4
4 × 2 = 8
4 × 3 = 12
4 × 4 = 16
4 × 5 = 20
4 × 6 = 24
4 × 7 = 28
4 × 8 = 32
4 × 9 = 36
4 × 10 = 40
4 × 11 = 44
4 × 12 = 48

5

5 × 1 = 5
5 × 2 = 10
5 × 3 = 15
5 × 4 = 20
5 × 5 = 25
5 × 6 = 30
5 × 7 = 35
5 × 8 = 40
5 × 9 = 45
5 × 10 = 50
5 × 11 = 55
5 × 12 = 60

6

6 × 1 = 6
6 × 2 = 12
6 × 3 = 18
6 × 4 = 24
6 × 5 = 30
6 × 6 = 36
6 × 7 = 42
6 × 8 = 48
6 × 9 = 54
6 × 10 = 60
6 × 11 = 66
6 × 12 = 72

7

7 × 1 = 7
7 × 2 = 14
7 × 3 = 21
7 × 4 = 28
7 × 5 = 35
7 × 6 = 42
7 × 7 = 49
7 × 8 = 56
7 × 9 = 63
7 × 10 = 70
7 × 11 = 77
7 × 12 = 84

8

8 × 1 = 8
8 × 2 = 16
8 × 3 = 24
8 × 4 = 32
8 × 5 = 40
8 × 6 = 48
8 × 7 = 56
8 × 8 = 64
8 × 9 = 72
8 × 10 = 80
8 × 11 = 88
8 × 12 = 96

9

9 × 1 = 9
9 × 2 = 18
9 × 3 = 27
9 × 4 = 36
9 × 5 = 45
9 × 6 = 54
9 × 7 = 63
9 × 8 = 72
9 × 9 = 81
9 × 10 = 90
9 × 11 = 99
9 × 12 = 108

10

10 × 1 = 10
10 × 2 = 20
10 × 3 = 30
10 × 4 = 40
10 × 5 = 50
10 × 6 = 60
10 × 7 = 70
10 × 8 = 80
10 × 9 = 90
10 × 10 = 100
10 × 11 = 110
10 × 12 = 120

11

11 × 1 = 11
11 × 2 = 22
11 × 3 = 33
11 × 4 = 44
11 × 5 = 55
11 × 6 = 66
11 × 7 = 77
11 × 8 = 88
11 × 9 = 99
11 x 10 = 110
11 x 11 = 121
11 x 12 = 132

12

12 × 1 = 12
12 × 2 = 24
12 × 3 = 36
12 × 4 = 48
12 × 5 = 60
12 × 6 = 72
12 × 7 = 84
12 × 8 = 96
12 × 9 = 108
12 × 10 = 120
12 × 11 = 132
12 × 12 = 144

Warm up 1

x	2	4	8	12
8				
1				
9				
2				
12				
4				
10				
3				
11				
7				
6				
5				
Total				
Time =			Total =	

Warm-up 1 Answers

x	2	4	8	12
8	16	32	64	96
1	2	4	8	12
9	18	36	72	108
2	4	8	16	24
12	24	48	96	144
4	8	16	32	48
10	20	40	80	120
3	6	12	24	36
11	22	44	88	132
7	14	28	56	84
6	12	24	48	72
5	10	20	40	60

Warm up 2

x	3	6	9	11
8				
1				
10				
2				
11				
4				
6				
3				
9				
7				
5				
12				
Total				
Time =		Total =		

Warm up 2 Answers

x	3	6	9	11
8	24	48	72	88
1	3	6	9	11
10	30	60	90	110
2	6	12	18	22
11	33	66	99	121
4	12	24	36	44
6	18	36	54	66
3	9	18	27	33
9	27	54	81	99
7	21	42	63	77
5	15	30	45	55
12	36	72	108	132

Warm up 3

	1	5	7	10
8				
2				
9				
3				
10				
4				
6				
5				
12				
7				
11				
1				
Total				
Time =		Total =		

Warm up 3 Answers

x	1	5	7	10
8	8	40	56	80
2	2	10	14	20
9	9	45	63	90
3	3	15	21	30
10	10	50	70	100
4	4	20	28	40
6	6	30	42	60
5	5	25	35	50
12	12	60	84	120
7	7	35	49	70
11	11	55	77	110
1	1	5	7	10

TIMES TABLES GRIDS

INSTRUCTIONS FOR THE GRIDS

Let's embark on a maths adventure through the 1-12 times tables! 🚀

Imagine your grid as a treasure map filled with multiplication secrets. Each row and column leads to hidden answers waiting to be uncovered.
As you explore, multiply the chosen row and column numbers together. It's like being a fearless number explorer! 🕵️❌

Where the row and column meet, you've found a secret answer 🔻. Record it in the box; it's like discovering buried treasure! 💲☠️

Now, mark your grid with special ticks (✔️). If you need help or want to double-check, find answers at the back of your book, but only look at your completed grid! 📄🔍

Here's a handy tip: use a different colour to highlight any answers that need correction. It makes them stand out! ✨🔢🌈

Let's make this maths adventure exciting and full of curiosity! 🚀🌈⭐

HOW TO USE THE GRID

Example												
x	1	2	3	4	5	6	7	8	9	10	11	12
1	1	2	3	4	5	6	7	8	9	10	11	12
2	2	4	6	8	10	12	14	16	18	20	22	24
3	3	6	9	12	15	18	24	24	27	30	33	36
4	4	8	12	16	20	24	28	32	36	40	44	48
5	5	10	15	20	25	30	35	40	45	50	55	60
6	6	12	18	24	30	36	42	48	54	60	66	72
7	7	14	21	28	35	42	49	56	63	70	77	84
8	8	16	24	32	40	52	56	64	72	80	88	96
9	9	18	27	36	45	54	63	72	81	90	99	108
10	10	20	30	40	50	60	70	80	90	100	110	120
11	11	22	33	44	55	66	77	88	99	110	121	132
12	12	24	36	48	60	72	84	96	108	120	132	144

Time = 10.78   Total = 142

PINPOINT THE BLUNDER, SO YOU CAN NAIL IT NEXT ROUND.

RECORD YOUR GRID-CONQUERING TIME!

ADD UP THOSE POINTS AND SCRIBBLE THEM DOWN!

INSTRUCTIONS FOR SELF-ASSESSING

Let's dive into the exciting part - Self-Assessment, Reflection, and Goal-Setting! 🚀 Use your colouring pens ✏️ to fill in stars and faces, showing your mastery over each question. More happy faces, more power to you! ☺️

Check off ✅ you understood times tables, and note the tricky ones 🔧. With a bit of help, set your improvement goals in the final box. Remember, setting goals is your roadmap to success!

Embrace the Marvellous Mistake Mission! Choose three notable errors and rewrite each five times. Focus prevents confusion and turns blunders into wisdom! Stuck? Set a new mini-goal! It's self-coaching towards mastering, say, the 5 times table. 🤸

By acknowledging mistakes, practicing, and goal-setting, you're stepping into your maths magician shoes! 🎩 ✨ Your colourful corrections and highlights will make your learning journey shine! ⭐ Ready to be a multiplication master? The adventure awaits! 🎢

HOW TO USE SELF-ASSESSMENT

TOGETHER,
LET'S CREATE A
GALAXY OF
TRIUMPHS!

CELEBRATE
YOUR
EMOTIONS
WITH A
FUNKY
CHECKMARK
☑ AND JAZZ
IT UP WITH A
COMMENT!

EXPRESS
YOURSELF!
✦ CHOOSE
AND
COLOUR A
FACE TO
MATCH
YOUR
MOOD. 😊

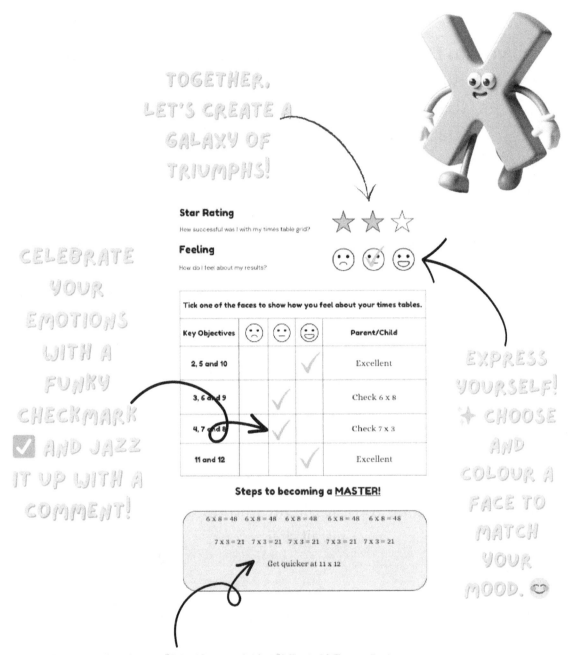

Star Rating

How successful was I with my times table grid?

★ ★ ☆

Feeling

How do I feel about my results?

☹ 😐 😃

Tick one of the faces to show how you feel about your times tables.

Key Objectives	☹	😐	😃	Parent/Child
2, 5 and 10			✓	Excellent
3, 6 and 9		✓		Check 6 x 8
4, 7 and 8		✓		Check 7 x 3
11 and 12			✓	Excellent

Steps to becoming a <u>MASTER!</u>

6 X 8 = 48   6 X 8 = 48   6 X 8 = 48   6 X 8 = 48   6 X 8 = 48

7 X 3 = 21   7 X 3 = 21   7 X 3 = 21   7 X 3 = 21   7 X 3 = 21

Get quicker at 11 x 12

WHEN SETBACKS HIT, SHAKE THEM OFF
AND GET CREATIVE! WRITE DOWN YOUR
IDEAS FIVE TIMES – IT'S A MINI MAKEOVER
FOR YOUR THOUGHTS!

Grid 1

x	4	9	3	12	7	10	6	5	8	1	11	2
8												
2												
9												
3												
6												
1												
11												
4												
7												
10												
5												
12												

Grid 1 Answers

x	4	9	3	12	7	10	6	5	8	1	11	2
8	32	72	24	96	56	80	48	40	64	8	88	16
2	8	18	6	24	14	20	12	10	16	2	22	4
9	36	81	27	108	63	90	54	45	72	9	99	18
3	12	27	9	36	21	30	18	15	24	3	33	6
6	24	54	18	72	42	60	36	30	48	6	66	12
1	4	9	3	12	7	10	6	5	8	1	11	2
11	44	99	33	132	77	110	66	55	88	11	121	22
4	16	36	12	48	28	40	24	20	32	4	44	8
7	28	63	21	84	49	70	42	35	56	7	77	14
10	40	90	30	120	70	100	60	50	80	10	110	20
5	20	45	15	60	35	50	30	25	40	5	55	10
12	48	108	36	144	84	120	72	60	96	12	132	24

Self Assessment

Star Rating

How successful was I with my times table grid?

Feeling

How do I feel about my results?

Tick one of the faces to show how you feel about your times tables.				
Key Objectives	🙁	😐	🙂	**Parent/Child**
2, 5 and 10				
3, 6 and 9				
4, 7 and 8				
11 and 12				

Steps to becoming a __MASTER!__

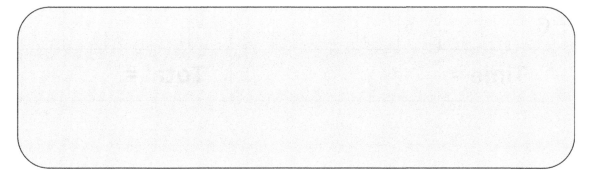

Grid 2

x	6	1	11	3	8	9	2	7	4	12	10	5
8												
2												
7												
9												
5												
4												
12												
1												
10												
3												
11												
6												

Time =   Total =

Grid 2 Answers

x	6	1	11	3	8	9	2	7	4	12	10	5
8	48	8	88	24	64	72	16	56	32	96	80	40
2	12	2	22	6	16	18	4	14	8	24	20	10
7	42	7	77	21	56	63	14	49	28	84	70	35
9	54	9	99	27	72	81	18	63	36	108	90	45
5	30	5	55	15	40	45	10	35	20	60	50	25
4	24	4	44	12	32	36	8	28	16	48	40	20
12	72	12	132	36	96	108	24	84	48	144	120	60
1	6	1	11	3	8	9	2	7	4	12	10	5
10	60	10	110	30	80	90	20	70	40	120	100	50
3	18	3	33	9	24	27	6	21	12	36	30	15
11	66	11	121	33	88	99	22	77	44	132	110	55
6	36	6	66	18	48	54	12	42	24	72	60	30

Self Assessment

Star Rating

How successful was I with my times table grid?

Feeling

How do I feel about my results?

Tick one of the faces to show how you feel about your times tables.				
Key Objectives	☹	😐	😃	**Parent/Child**
2, 5 and 10				
3, 6 and 9				
4, 7 and 8				
11 and 12				

Steps to becoming a <u>MASTER!</u>

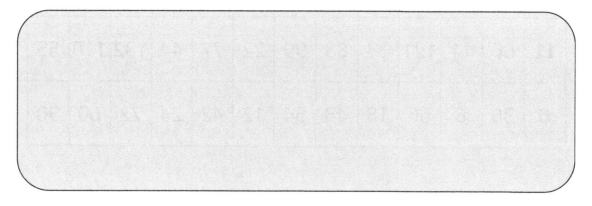

Grid 3

x	9	8	11	3	10	5	6	4	1	2	12	7
3												
5												
7												
1												
8												
4												
12												
9												
2												
10												
6												
11												

Time =   Total =

Grid 3 Answers

x	9	8	11	3	10	5	6	4	1	2	12	7
3	27	24	33	9	30	15	18	12	3	6	36	21
5	45	40	55	15	50	25	30	20	5	10	60	35
7	63	56	77	21	70	35	42	28	7	14	84	49
1	9	8	11	3	10	5	6	4	1	2	12	7
8	72	64	88	24	80	40	48	32	8	16	96	56
4	36	32	44	12	40	20	24	16	4	8	48	28
12	108	96	132	36	120	60	72	48	12	24	144	84
9	81	72	99	27	90	45	54	36	9	18	108	63
2	18	16	22	6	20	10	12	8	2	4	24	14
10	90	80	110	30	100	50	60	40	10	20	120	70
6	54	48	66	18	60	30	36	24	6	12	72	42
11	99	88	121	33	110	55	66	44	11	22	132	77

Self Assessment

Star Rating

How successful was I with my times table grid?

Feeling

How do I feel about my results?

Tick one of the faces to show how you feel about your times tables.			
Key Objectives	😕	😐	😀	Parent/Child
2, 5 and 10				
3, 6 and 9				
4, 7 and 8				
11 and 12				

Steps to becoming a <u>MASTER!</u>

Grid 4

x	11	3	5	9	6	10	1	8	7	2	4	12
2												
8												
1												
6												
9												
4												
7												
10												
12												
3												
5												
11												

Time =   Total =

213

Grid 4 Answers

x	11	3	5	9	6	10	1	8	7	2	4	12
2	22	6	10	18	12	20	2	16	14	4	8	24
8	88	24	40	72	48	80	8	64	56	16	32	96
1	11	3	5	9	6	10	1	8	7	2	4	12
6	66	18	30	54	36	60	6	48	42	12	24	72
9	99	27	45	81	54	90	9	72	63	18	36	108
4	44	12	20	36	24	40	4	32	28	8	16	48
7	77	21	35	63	42	70	7	56	49	14	28	84
10	110	30	50	90	60	100	10	80	70	20	40	120
12	132	36	60	108	72	120	12	96	84	24	48	144
3	33	9	15	27	18	30	3	24	21	6	12	36
5	55	15	25	45	30	50	5	40	35	10	20	60
11	121	33	55	99	66	110	11	88	77	22	44	132

Self Assessment

Star Rating

How successful was I with my times table grid?

Feeling

How do I feel about my results?

Tick one of the faces to show how you feel about your times tables.			
Key Objectives	😕	😐	😀	**Parent/Child**
2, 5 and 10				
3, 6 and 9				
4, 7 and 8				
11 and 12				

Steps to becoming a MASTER!

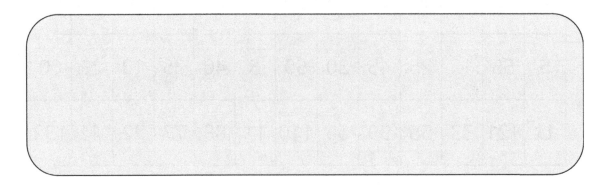

Grid 5

x	10	8	3	5	7	11	6	9	1	2	12	4
7												
4												
9												
2												
6												
1												
12												
5												
8												
3												
11												
10												

Time =   Total =

Grid 5 Answers

x	10	8	3	5	7	11	6	9	1	2	12	4
7	70	56	21	35	49	77	42	63	7	14	84	28
4	40	32	12	20	28	44	24	36	4	8	48	16
9	90	72	27	45	63	99	54	81	9	18	108	36
2	20	16	6	10	14	22	12	18	2	4	24	8
6	60	48	18	30	42	66	36	54	6	12	72	24
1	10	8	3	5	7	11	6	9	1	2	12	4
12	120	96	36	60	84	132	72	108	12	24	144	48
5	50	40	15	25	35	55	30	45	5	10	60	20
8	80	64	24	40	56	88	48	72	8	16	96	32
3	30	24	9	15	21	33	18	27	3	6	36	12
11	110	88	33	55	77	121	66	99	11	22	132	44
10	100	80	30	50	70	110	60	90	10	20	120	40

Self Assessment

Star Rating

How successful was I with my times table grid?

Feeling

How do I feel about my results?

Tick one of the faces to show how you feel about your times tables.				
Key Objectives	☹	😐	😀	**Parent/Child**
2, 5 and 10				
3, 6 and 9				
4, 7 and 8				
11 and 12				

Steps to becoming a MASTER!

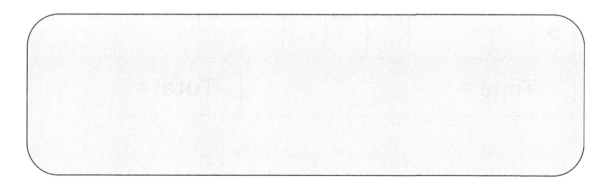

Grid 6

x	2	7	4	5	9	8	1	3	12	11	6	10
8												
4												
9												
11												
2												
6												
3												
1												
12												
10												
7												
5												

Time =   Total =

Grid 6 Answers

x	2	7	4	5	9	8	1	3	12	11	6	10
8	16	56	32	40	72	64	8	24	96	88	48	80
4	8	28	16	20	36	32	4	12	48	44	24	40
9	18	63	36	45	81	72	9	27	108	99	54	90
11	22	77	44	55	99	88	11	33	132	121	66	110
2	4	14	8	10	18	16	2	6	24	22	12	20
6	12	42	24	30	54	48	6	18	72	66	36	60
3	6	21	12	15	27	24	3	9	36	33	18	30
1	2	7	4	5	9	8	1	3	12	11	6	10
12	24	84	48	60	108	96	12	36	144	132	72	120
10	20	70	40	50	90	80	10	30	120	110	60	100
7	14	49	28	35	63	56	7	21	84	77	42	70
5	10	35	20	25	45	40	5	15	60	55	30	50

Self Assessment

Star Rating

How successful was I with my times table grid?

Feeling

How do I feel about my results?

Tick one of the faces to show how you feel about your times tables.				
Key Objectives	😞	😐	😀	Parent/Child
2, 5 and 10				
3, 6 and 9				
4, 7 and 8				
11 and 12				

Steps to becoming a __MASTER!__

Grid 7

x	10	6	11	2	5	12	9	1	7	3	4	8
2												
4												
1												
6												
8												
3												
9												
12												
5												
7												
11												
10												

Time =   Total =

Grid 7 Answers

x	10	6	11	2	5	12	9	1	7	3	4	8
2	20	12	22	4	10	24	18	2	14	6	8	16
4	40	24	44	8	20	48	36	4	28	12	16	32
1	10	6	11	2	5	12	9	1	7	3	4	8
6	60	36	66	12	30	72	54	6	42	18	24	48
8	80	48	88	16	40	96	72	8	56	24	32	64
3	30	18	33	6	15	36	27	3	21	9	12	24
9	90	54	99	18	45	108	81	9	63	27	36	72
12	120	72	132	24	60	144	108	12	84	36	48	96
5	50	30	55	10	25	60	45	5	35	15	20	40
7	70	42	77	14	35	84	63	7	49	21	28	56
11	110	66	121	22	55	132	99	11	77	33	44	88
10	100	60	110	20	50	120	90	10	70	30	40	80

Self Assessment

Star Rating

How successful was I with my times table grid?

Feeling

How do I feel about my results?

Tick one of the faces to show how you feel about your times tables.				
Key Objectives	☹	😐	😀	Parent/Child
2, 5 and 10				
3, 6 and 9				
4, 7 and 8				
11 and 12				

Steps to becoming a MASTER!

Grid 8

x	5	12	3	9	2	7	11	6	1	10	8	4
3												
1												
9												
6												
12												
7												
4												
8												
11												
2												
10												
5												

Time =   Total =

Grid 8 Answers

x	5	12	3	9	2	7	11	6	1	10	8	4
3	15	36	9	27	6	21	33	18	3	30	24	12
1	5	12	3	9	2	7	11	6	1	10	8	4
9	45	108	27	81	18	63	99	54	9	90	72	36
6	30	72	18	54	12	42	66	36	6	60	48	24
12	60	144	36	108	24	84	132	72	12	120	96	48
7	35	84	21	63	14	49	77	42	7	70	56	28
4	20	48	12	36	8	28	44	24	4	40	32	16
8	40	96	24	72	16	56	88	48	8	80	64	32
11	55	132	33	99	22	77	121	66	11	110	88	44
2	10	24	6	18	4	14	22	12	2	20	16	8
10	50	120	30	90	20	70	110	60	10	100	80	40
5	25	60	15	45	10	35	55	30	5	50	40	20

Self Assessment

Star Rating

How successful was I with my times table grid?

Feeling

How do I feel about my results?

Tick one of the faces to show how you feel about your times tables.			
Key Objectives	 ☹	😐	😀	**Parent/Child**
2, 5 and 10				
3, 6 and 9				
4, 7 and 8				
11 and 12				

Steps to becoming a MASTER!

Grid 9

x	11	4	7	1	12	9	5	8	6	3	10	2
5												
8												
1												
6												
3												
9												
7												
10												
2												
12												
4												
11												

Time =   Total =

Grid 9 Answers

x	11	4	7	1	12	9	5	8	6	3	10	2
5	55	20	35	5	60	45	25	40	30	15	50	10
8	88	32	56	8	96	72	40	64	48	24	80	16
1	11	4	7	1	12	9	5	8	6	3	10	2
6	66	24	42	6	72	54	30	48	36	18	60	12
3	33	12	21	3	36	27	15	24	18	9	30	6
9	99	36	63	9	108	81	45	72	54	27	90	18
7	77	28	49	7	84	63	35	56	42	21	70	14
10	110	40	70	10	120	90	50	80	60	30	100	20
2	22	8	14	2	24	18	10	16	12	6	20	4
12	132	48	84	12	144	108	60	96	72	36	120	24
4	44	16	28	4	48	36	20	32	24	12	40	8
11	121	44	77	11	132	99	55	88	66	33	110	22

Self Assessment

Star Rating

How successful was I with my times table grid?

Feeling

How do I feel about my results?

Tick one of the faces to show how you feel about your times tables.			
Key Objectives	☹	😐	🙂	**Parent/Child**
2, 5 and 10				
3, 6 and 9				
4, 7 and 8				
11 and 12				

Steps to becoming a <u>MASTER!</u>

Grid 10

x	6	8	12	5	4	7	1	11	3	2	9	10
3												
11												
2												
10												
8												
7												
5												
1												
12												
9												
4												
6												

Time =   Total =

Grid 10 Answers

x	6	8	12	5	4	7	1	11	3	2	9	10
3	18	24	36	15	12	21	3	33	9	6	27	30
11	66	88	132	55	44	77	11	121	33	22	99	110
2	12	16	24	10	8	14	2	22	6	4	18	20
10	60	80	120	50	40	70	10	110	30	20	90	100
8	48	64	96	40	32	56	8	88	24	16	72	80
7	42	56	84	35	28	49	7	77	21	14	63	70
5	30	40	60	25	20	35	5	55	15	10	45	50
1	6	8	12	5	4	7	1	11	3	2	9	10
12	72	96	144	60	48	84	12	132	36	24	108	120
9	54	72	108	45	36	63	9	99	27	18	81	90
4	24	32	48	20	16	28	4	44	12	8	36	40
6	36	48	72	30	24	42	6	66	18	12	54	60

Self Assessment

Star Rating

How successful was I with my times table grid?

Feeling

How do I feel about my results?

Tick one of the faces to show how you feel about your times tables.				
Key Objectives	☹	😐	🙂	**Parent/Child**
2, 5 and 10				
3, 6 and 9				
4, 7 and 8				
11 and 12				

Steps to becoming a <u>MASTER!</u>

Grid 11

x	10	3	9	11	1	8	2	4	5	7	12	6
7												
11												
5												
4												
1												
6												
2												
8												
9												
3												
10												
12												

Time =   Total =

Grid 11 Answers

x	10	3	9	11	1	8	2	4	5	7	12	6
7	70	21	63	77	7	56	14	28	35	49	84	42
11	110	33	99	121	11	88	22	44	55	77	132	66
5	50	15	45	55	5	40	10	20	25	35	60	30
4	40	12	36	44	4	32	8	16	20	28	48	24
1	10	3	9	11	1	8	2	4	5	7	12	6
6	60	18	54	66	6	48	12	24	30	42	72	36
2	20	6	18	22	2	16	4	8	10	14	24	12
8	80	24	72	88	8	64	16	32	40	56	96	48
9	90	27	81	99	9	72	18	36	45	63	108	54
3	30	9	27	33	3	24	6	12	15	21	36	18
10	100	30	90	110	10	80	20	40	50	70	120	60
12	120	36	108	132	12	96	24	48	60	84	144	72

Self Assessment

Star Rating

How successful was I with my times table grid?

Feeling

How do I feel about my results?

Tick one of the faces to show how you feel about your times tables.				
Key Objectives	☹	😐	😀	Parent/Child
2, 5 and 10				
3, 6 and 9				
4, 7 and 8				
11 and 12				

Steps to becoming a **MASTER!**

Grid 12

x	6	11	5	9	1	8	4	3	12	2	7	10
7												
12												
8												
1												
6												
3												
4												
10												
9												
11												
2												
5												

Time =   Total =

Grid 12 Answers

x	6	11	5	9	1	8	4	3	12	2	7	10
7	42	77	35	63	7	56	28	21	84	14	49	70
12	72	132	60	108	12	96	48	36	144	24	84	120
8	48	88	40	72	8	64	32	24	96	16	56	80
1	6	11	5	9	1	8	4	3	12	2	7	10
6	36	66	30	54	6	48	24	18	72	12	42	60
3	18	33	15	27	3	24	12	9	36	6	21	30
4	24	44	20	36	4	32	16	12	48	8	28	40
10	60	110	50	90	10	80	40	30	120	20	70	100
9	54	99	45	81	9	72	36	27	108	18	63	90
11	66	121	55	99	11	88	44	33	132	22	77	110
2	12	22	10	18	2	16	8	6	24	4	14	20
5	30	55	25	45	5	40	20	15	60	10	35	50

Self Assessment

Star Rating

How successful was I with my times table grid?

Feeling

How do I feel about my results?

Tick one of the faces to show how you feel about your times tables.			
Key Objectives	😞	😐	😀	Parent/Child
2, 5 and 10				
3, 6 and 9				
4, 7 and 8				
11 and 12				

Steps to becoming a **MASTER!**

REVIEW

 Leave Your Mark with Sakura Learning!

Thank you for choosing our Super Times Tables Book! We're excited to be part of your child's journey to mastering times tables from 1-12. Scan the QR code below to leave a review and help other parents choose the best educational resources!

Your review matters! It guides parents, motivates our team, drives continuous improvement, and builds a supportive community. Together, let's empower children to excel in maths and love learning!

Scan the QR code to leave your review now!

Time Tables Drills The Fun Way: Over 100 Days of Multiplication Tests

Boost your multiplication skills with a fun, engaging method! Designed by a former head of maths with over 20 years of teaching experience, this book is more than just a workbook—it's a transformative learning tool. Embrace a growth mindset, assess your progress with provided answer keys, and turn every mistake into a learning opportunity. Master multiplication the engaging way. Scan the QR below to get your book today!

Made in the USA
Las Vegas, NV
06 June 2024

90771524R00142